READINGS ON

THE
METAMORPHOSIS

OTHER TITLES IN THE GREENHAVEN PRESS
LITERARY COMPANION SERIES:

WORLD AUTHORS

Fyodor Dostoyevsky
Homer
Sophocles

WORLD LITERATURE

All Quiet on the Western
  Front
Antigone
Candide
Crime and Punishment
Cry, the Beloved Country
Cyrano de Bergerac
The Diary of a Young Girl
A Doll's House
Medea
Night
One Day in the Life of
  Ivan Denisovich
The Stranger

THE GREENHAVEN PRESS
Literary Companion
TO WORLD LITERATURE

READINGS ON

THE METAMORPHOSIS

Hayley Mitchell Haugen, *Book Editor*

Daniel Leone, *President*
Bonnie Szumski, *Publisher*
Marla Ryan, *Series Editor*

Greenhaven Press, Inc., San Diego, CA

Every effort has been made to trace the owners of copy-righted material. The articles in this volume may have been edited for content, length, and/or reading level. The titles have been changed to enhance the editorial purpose. Those interested in locating the original source will find the complete citation on the first page of each article.

Library of Congress Cataloging-in-Publication Data

Readings on The metamorphosis / Hayley Mitchell Haugen, book editor.
        p. cm. —
    Includes bibliographical references and index.
    ISBN 0-7377-0440-3 (lib. bdg. : alk. paper) —
ISBN 0-7377-0439-X (pbk. bdg. : alk. paper)
    1. Kafka, Franz, 1883–1924. Verwandlung. I. Title:
The Metamorphosis. II. Haugen, Hayley Mitchell, 1968–

PT2621.A26 V458 2002
833'.912—dc21

                                                    2001033973

Cover photo: © Bettmann/CORBIS

"The Metamorphosis *is not a confession, although it is—in a certain sense—an indiscretion. . . . It is perhaps delicate and discreet to talk about the bugs in one's own family.*"

—Franz Kafka
from *Conversations with Kafka*
by Gustav Janouch

CONTENTS

tendency to project psychological drama into a theological perspective.

Chapter 2: Themes in *The Metamorphosis*

Chapter 3: The Psychology of *The Metamorphosis*

Chapter 4: Interpretive Criticism About *The Metamorphosis*

FOREWORD

> *"'Tis the good reader that*
> *makes the good book."*
>
> Ralph Waldo Emerson

The story's bare facts are simple: The captain, an old and scarred seafarer, walks with a peg leg made of whale ivory. He relentlessly drives his crew to hunt the world's oceans for the great white whale that crippled him. After a long search, the ship encounters the whale and a fierce battle ensues. Finally the captain drives his harpoon into the whale, but the harpoon line catches the captain about the neck and drags him to his death.

A simple story, a straightforward plot—yet, since the 1851 publication of Herman Melville's *Moby-Dick*, readers and critics have found many meanings in the struggle between Captain Ahab and the whale. To some, the novel is a cautionary tale that depicts how Ahab's obsession with revenge leads to his insanity and death. Others believe that the whale represents the unknowable secrets of the universe and that Ahab is a tragic hero who dares to challenge fate by attempting to discover this knowledge. Perhaps Melville intended Ahab as a criticism of Americans' tendency to become involved in well-intentioned but irrational causes. Or did Melville model Ahab after himself, letting his fictional character express his anger at what he perceived as a cruel and distant god?

Although literary critics disagree over the meaning of *Moby-Dick*, readers do not need to choose one particular interpretation in order to gain an understanding of Melville's novel. Instead, by examining various analyses, they can gain numerous insights into the issues that lie under the surface of the basic plot. Studying the writings of literary critics can also aid readers in making their own assessments of *Moby-Dick* and other literary works and in developing analytical thinking skills.

The Greenhaven Literary Companion Series was created with these goals in mind. Designed for young adults, this unique anthology series provides an engaging and comprehensive introduction to literary analysis and criticism. The essays included in the Literary Companion Series are chosen for their accessibility to a young adult audience and are expertly edited in consideration of both the reading and comprehension levels of this audience. In addition, each essay is introduced by a concise summation that presents the contributing writer's main themes and insights. Every anthology in the Literary Companion Series contains a varied selection of critical essays that cover a wide time span and express diverse views. Wherever possible, primary sources are represented through excerpts from authors' notebooks, letters, and journals and through contemporary criticism.

Each title in the Literary Companion Series pays careful consideration to the historical context of the particular author or literary work. In-depth biographies and detailed chronologies reveal important aspects of authors' lives and emphasize the historical events and social milieu that influenced their writings. To facilitate further research, every anthology includes primary and secondary source bibliographies of articles and/or books selected for their suitability for young adults. These engaging features make the Greenhaven Literary Companion series ideal for introducing students to literary analysis in the classroom or as a library resource for young adults researching the world's great authors and literature.

Exceptional in its focus on young adults, the Greenhaven Literary Companion Series strives to present literary criticism in a compelling and accessible format. Every title in the series is intended to spark readers' interest in leading American and world authors, to help them broaden their understanding of literature, and to encourage them to formulate their own analyses of the literary works that they read. It is the editors' hope that young adult readers will find these anthologies to be true companions in their study of literature.

INTRODUCTION

Beginning in 1908, when he first published selections from his novel *Amerika*, and ending in 1924, when he died at the age of forty-one, Franz Kafka's career as a writer spanned a mere sixteen years. At the time of his death, many of what are now known as his major novels had not been published, and Kafka himself was relatively unknown outside of the realm of German literature. Today, however, Kafka is not only considered the most significant writer to emerge from the Prague Circle, a group of German-Jewish writers that formed in the early 1880s and remained active until the end of World War I, he is celebrated as a central figure in all of twentieth-century literature. In light of his important standing in the literary canon today, it is surprising to learn that his works, had he had his way, may have never survived to be read at all.

Suffering from tuberculosis and nearing his death, Franz Kafka released much of his written works to his friend and future editor and biographer Max Brod. His instructions to Brod specified that five books and two stories (*The Judgement, The Stoker, The Metamorphosis, In the Penal Colony, Meditation,* "A Country Doctor," and the "The Hunger Artist") should be preserved, but not reprinted. Biographer Frederick R. Karl notes that Kafka "simply felt that while [these works] were 'valid' for his time and place, they were not to be passed on to future generations. He could not, of course, control this, nor could Brod, since once published, the pieces' future belonged to publishers."[1] Kafka requested the remainder of his work—his diaries, letters, unfinished manuscripts, work in periodicals, and other papers—be burned.

Many Kafka critics and biographers have interpreted Kafka's request to have his work destroyed as a symptom of his perfectionism, his disappointment with the quality of most of his work. Karl, however, argues that Kafka's request was really an act of pride, an enormous vanity. "If he truly wished everything except a few items burned, then in the time remaining he would have made the effort himself," Karl writes. "By leaving the task to Brod, he was, like pharaohs and other tyrants, creating a funeral pyre in his honor."[2]

Once destroyed, Kafka's work would remain his alone. In death, Karl notes, Kafka could keep his work to himself, away from the contamination of others' eyes and opinions. Max Brod, however, is of those who feel Kafka desired his works destroyed simply because they did not meet with the stringent standards by which he judged himself. He did not have time, Brod says, to worry what others thought of him:

> For he was wholly occupied with the striving for the highest ethical pinnacle a man can attain—a pinnacle which in truth scarcely can be attained. He was filled with a drive, intensified to the point of pain and semi-madness, not to brook any vice in himself, any lie any self-deception, nor any offence against his fellow men—this passion for perfection often took the form of self-humiliation, since Kafka saw his own weaknesses as though under a microscope, magnified to many times their size.[3]

That Max Brod did not heed his friend's wish that his body of work die with him, and that Kafka's publishers saw fit to reprint those works published during his lifetime, is to the benefit of all students of literature. Unarguably the most famous of Kafka's works, *The Metamorphosis* has become the most widely anthologized and most frequently analyzed of all his literary efforts. Numerous books and hundreds of articles have been devoted to the critical analysis of the novella alone.

The essays in this volume explore the technical, thematic, and psychological forces at work in *The Metamorphosis.* Some contemporary critics represented here explore Kafka's craft, from his use of formal structure in the novella to the meaningful imagery and symbolism present throughout the work. Other critics focus on thematic issues, such as the roles of self-alienation or banishment in the story, or on psychological concerns, including Gregor Samsa's loss of male identity and the dangers of family dependency. In all, readers will find that these topics and many others in this collection offer a varied and exciting introduction to criticism on Franz Kafka and *The Metamorphosis.*

NOTES

1. Excerpted from Frederick R. Karl, *Franz Kafka: Representative Man.* New York: Ticknor & Fields, 1991, p. 718.
2. Karl, *Franz Kafka: Representative Man,* p. 718.
3. Excerpted from Max Brod, *Franz Kafka: A Biography.* New York: Schocken Books, 1963, p. 214.

FRANZ KAFKA: A BIOGRAPHY

The first child of Hermann and Julie Kafka, upper middle class, German-speaking Jews living in Prague, Czechoslovakia, Franz Kafka was born on July 3, 1883. He was the eldest of four surviving children (two brothers died in infancy) and, along with his three sisters, was raised by nannies while his mother helped his father run a large, profitable dry-goods store. Of his two parents, Kafka's father had the most psychological effect on him. Hermann Kafka was successful, aggressive, and energetic. He was a tall, broad-shouldered, powerful man, and Franz felt overshadowed by both his imposing stature and business success throughout his life. Even at an early age, the diminutive, timid Franz exaggerated the role of his father to heroic proportions he could never live up to. "I remember, for instance, how we often used to get undressed in the same cubicle at the swimming bath," Kafka wrote to his father. "I was skinny, weak and slight, while you were big, strong and powerfully-built. I felt then that I was a thoroughly miserable specimen."[1]

In addition to feeling physically inadequate in his father's presence, Kafka felt his father took only a passing interest in his upbringing, interacting with him only at mealtimes. Looking for reassurance from his father that he was a good, worthy boy, Kafka instead felt bullied, taunted, and frightened by his father. Kafka later exposed these feelings in a "Letter to His Father," a lengthy autobiographical piece in which he explored his father's early influence in his life. "The 'Letter,'" Kafka's close friend and eventual biographer, Max Brod, writes, "recalls with uncanny penetration an insignificant punishment in earliest childhood, which was concerned anyhow with the child's moral rather than bodily welfare, and yet made an ineradicable impression on the son, because he recognized 'that I was such a mere nothing to him.'"[2] Indeed, Kafka captured his father's tyrannical behavior that led to his own sense of worthlessness, writing:

You had worked yourself up to such a position by your own strength, that you had unlimited confidence in your own opinion. . . . From your armchair you ruled the world. Your opinion was right, everybody else's was mad, eccentric, *meshuggah,* not normal. At the same time your self-confidence was so great that there was no need for you to be consistent, and yet you were always right. You often even happened to have no opinion whatever on a subject, in which case any possible opinion on the subject must, without exception, be wrong. You could swear at the Czechs, for example, and then at the Germans, and then at the Jews, not for any particular reason but for every reason, and in the end there was nobody left but yourself. For me you developed the bewildering effect that all tyrants have whose might is founded not on reason, but on their own person.[3]

Hermann Kafka's authority over his son would determine where he worked and who he dated and contribute greatly to Kafka's feelings of inadequacy and helplessness, not unlike those of Gregor Samsa in *The Metamorphosis.* His father's authoritative influence affected the themes of many of Kafka's other writings as well. Biographer Allan Blunden notes, for instance, that in Kafka's longer works, *The Trial* and *The Castle,* "images of distant and arbitrary regimes, will later spring from the same soil [as Kafka's "Letter to His Father"]: but this is no longer parental authority, but totalitarianism writ small."[4]

Biographer Walter Sokel notes that while Kafka's authoritative father provided him with images of tyranny that would prove to be important in his writings, Kafka saw himself less like his aggressive father and more like the Talmudic scholars and rabbis on his mother's side of the family—reflective, introverted, and timid. Eventually feeling that he could never rival his father as a successful businessman, Kafka turned inward instead, to the quiet life of the writer. Sokel writes that Kafka's "only hope left to him was, as he put it, to find a spot on the world's map that his father's enormous shadow had not reached—and that spot was literature."[5] And Kafka embraced this life of literature at an early age, writing plays for his sisters to perform, and becoming an avid reader.

KAFKA'S EDUCATION AND WORK EXPERIENCE

From 1893 to 1901, Kafka attended German preparatory schools in Prague and spoke German, the language of the elite class, rather than Czech. He was successful in his studies, which included classes in Latin, Greek, and history. During these years he also began writing short prose sketches, which were destroyed before Kafka gained critical acclaim for his later works.

In 1901 Kafka graduated from the German State Gymnasium and went on to attend Karl-Ferdinand University, where he studied law and began formal studies in German literature. During this time at the university, he met Brod, a writer a year younger than himself who had already achieved some acclaim for his work. Brod fondly remembers his friendship with Kafka in those days: "The richness of his thoughts, which he generally uttered in a cheerful tone, made him, to put it on the lowest level, one of the most amusing men I have ever met, in spite of his shyness, in spite of his quietness. He talked very little; when there were a lot of people he often didn't speak for hours on end. But when he did say something, everybody had to listen immediately, because it was always something full of meat, something that hit the nail on the head."[6]

Realizing right away that Kafka was a man of special talent, Brod strove to help him become successful through his writing. Brod was especially influential in that he not only urged Kafa to write, but also introduced him to prominent people in the literary world and arranged for the first publications of his work. With Brod's encouragement, Kafka became more serious about his writing and completed "Description of a Struggle," the first of his stories that remain in existence today, before he graduated from college.

In June 1906, Kafka graduated with a doctorate in law. Although he trained for some time to practice criminal and civil law in Prague, he yearned for a work situation that would allow him to develop his craft as a writer. He discovered this opportunity in 1908, when he began working at the Workers' Accident Insurance Institute. His work hours from 8:00 A.M. to 2:00 P.M. afforded him the free time he needed to write. However, in 1911 Kafka's father insisted that Kafka help manage his brother-in-law's asbestos factory in the afternoons, and this endeavor occupied much of Kafka's free time until the factory closed in 1917. Without the time and energy to put into his creative endeavors, Kafka grew lethargic, despondent, and prone to thoughts of suicide.

BROADENING HORIZONS

Despite his lack of free time for writing during the six years that he managed the asbestos factory, Kafka continued to grow as an artist as more literary and cultural opportunities arose for him during this time. In addition to traveling to Paris, Italy, and Switzerland with Max Brod and keeping extensive travel diaries, in 1911 Kafka also gained a new interest in Yiddish theater. He attended many performances of a Yiddish theater company in Prague and became close friends with Isaac Löwy, a leading actor in the group, who was instrumental in helping Kafka reconnect with his Jewish roots. "Hitherto," Sokel writes, "his attitude toward Judaism had been one of indifference. He found the conventionalized remnants of Jewish custom and religion in his family and social milieu pathetic and laughable."[7] Kafka began to study Jewish folklore during this time, and, a few years later, also undertook a study of Hebrew and the Old Testament. He even considered immigrating to Palestine to further explore his Jewish roots.

In 1912 Kafka's literary horizons broadened yet again, when Brod convinced him that he should strive to publish his writing in book form and introduced him to publisher Ernst Rowohlt and Rowohlt's associate, Kurt Wolff. Wolff was especially taken by Kafka's work and soon became his publisher when he broke from Rowohlt and founded his own publishing house. The first of Kafka's book publications, *Meditation*—a collection of small vignettes, meditations, and impressions—appeared in January 1913.

KAFKA'S FIRST ENGAGEMENT AND THE OTHER WOMAN

As Kafka made advances in the realm of literature, he also made advances in the realm of love. Although Kafka never married, he was rarely at a loss for female companionship. During college he had affairs with barmaids, waitresses, and shopgirls. His first serious relationship, however, began in 1912, when he met Felice Bauer, a young woman from Berlin. The two began corresponding, generating over five hundred letters and cards between them over the course of their five-year relationship. Although Kafka spent much of his time with Bauer trying to convince her that he was an unfit partner for her, in part due to his distaste for physical intimacy, Kafka proposed in 1913, and the couple became engaged in Berlin in June 1914. Kafka wrote of marriage: "To get married, to found a family, to accept all the children that arrive, to maintain them in this uncertain world, and even to lead them a little on their way is, in my opinion, the utmost that a man can ever succeed in doing."[8] Marriage, however, was not something, in the end, that he could picture himself being successful at. Thus, one month after his engagement to Bauer, Kafka called off the wedding.

While Bauer and Kafka continued their correspondence after their breakup, Kafka also began communicating with Bauer's friend, Grete Bloch. In the beginning, Bloch acted as a kind of intermediary between Kafka and Bauer, as he was able to share his fears about marriage openly with Bloch. Soon, however, Kafka and Bloch began a short-lived affair unbeknownst to Bauer. Upon reading her diaries and letters some twenty-five years later, Max Brod would discover Bloch's claim of giving birth to Kafka's illegitimate son in 1914. Bloch writes that the boy died in 1921 at age seven, although concrete evidence of neither the birth nor the death has been discovered to date.

By 1915, Kafka had refocused his affections on Bauer, and in 1917, the two became engaged for the second time. This time the engagement lasted a few months, and the couple even went as far as choosing furniture for their future household. However, the wedding plans were again called off when Kafka suffered a hemorrhage of the lungs in August 1917 and was diagnosed with tuberculosis. Biographers agree that Kafka was relieved to find a way out of his second engagement. However, he did not take the news of his illness lightly. Of illness, Kafka once said to his friend, Gustav Janouch, "Good health is not a personal possession, to do what one likes with. It is property on loan, a grace. Most people do not realize this, so they have no hygienic economy. . . . Inquiries about one's health increase one's consciousness of dying, to which as a sick man I am particularly exposed."[9]

A BOOM IN LITERARY PRODUCTIVITY

Although his health was failing and his love affairs never led to any kind of permanent relationship, Kafka was successful in what mattered most to him during the years of his courtships with Bauer and Bloch: his writing. In fact, he wrote some of his most acclaimed work during that period. In September 1912, for example, he wrote *The Judgement* over a twenty-four-hour span, dedicating the story to Bauer. He considered the story his first piece of mature work and willingly shared it with his friends and family. It would remain what he considered his best work, his only piece of writing that continually pleased him.

Next, in November and December, he wrote *The Metamorphosis* and worked on *Amerika,* from which his story *The Stoker* was derived. *The Judgement, The Metamorphosis,* and *The Stoker* were published by Wolff within the next three years. In addition to these efforts and accomplishments, Kafka completed "Memoirs of the Kalda Railroad" and "In the Penal Colony," and began writing *The Trial* in 1914, working on it intermittently until 1916. During these years, he also began to receive critical acclaim for his work. His reputation as a writer grew in 1915, for instance, when he won the Theodor Fontane Prize, an award of 800 marks, for *The Stoker.*

A MOVE TO THE COUNTRY

Kafka's writing career burgeoned while his health continued to decline. Physically exhausted, he found it increasingly difficult to keep to his schedule of working at his job during the day and writing through the night. Thus, after receiving the diagnosis of his tuberculosis and breaking off his second engagement to Bauer, Kafka obtained an extended sick leave from the Workers' Accident Insurance Institute and moved to the country house of his favorite sister, Ottla, in Zürau, northwest of Prague. From the winter of 1917 through most of 1918 he remained there, purporting it to be a peaceful and productive time of his life. Taking advantage of the quiet countryside, Kafka spent his time reflecting on metaphysical and religious problems and studying Jewish legends and mystical lore in addition to other literature. Influenced by his readings in the country, Kafka wrote a number of aphorisms, collected in what he called *The Blue Octavo Notebooks,* a gathering of proverbs, musings, and sketches. Kafka's "The Great Wall of China," "A Country Doctor," and "The New Attorney," were also among the stories written during this period.

Before the year's end in 1918, Kafka, now age 35, returned to Prague and worked half-time at the insurance institute. He soon met Julie Wohryzek, and despite his ill health, the two became engaged in 1919. Wohryzek's father was a janitor and shoemaker, and Kafka's father vehemently disapproved of his relationship with her on the grounds that she was from a lower social class. Although the couple had already picked out an apartment to share, Kafka, being sufficiently shamed by his father, broke off the engagement a few days before the wedding ceremony.

His father's interference in his latest engagement moved Kafka to write "Letter to His Father" that same year. The long autobiographical piece condemns his father for the negative role he played in shaping Kafka's life. His father, however, never read the work, as Kafka's mother refused Kafka's request to deliver it to him.

THE ILLNESS ADVANCES

Upon his return to Prague in 1918, and up until his death in 1924, Kafka's illness demanded intermittent stays at various sanatoriums. The insurance institute granted these extended sick leaves as necessary. Kafka was still able to write during these periods, and between 1918 and 1921, for instance, he continued writing in his diary and working on his parables; he wrote "The Bucket Rider," and he completed the first draft of *The Castle.*

During one of these sick leaves at a sanatorium in Slovakia in 1920, Kafka began a correspondence with Milena Jesenská-Pollak, a Czech writer and intellectual who had translated a number of Kafka's works into Czech. She was the wife of Kafka's friend, Ernst Pollak. After separating from her husband because of his infidelities, Jesenská-Pollak began a brief affair with Kafka. While the letters of the pair suggest a deep level of emotional intimacy, as in his other relationships with women, Kafka remained fearful of physical contact. When his anxieties about having sex with Jesenská-Pollak grew and he evaded her desire for sexual encounters, she soon ended their affair. By 1923, when Jesenská-Pollak resumed her relationship with her former husband, she and Kafka had ceased corresponding with each other, having broken off their relationship during a final meeting in 1922.

His affair with Jesenská-Pollak over, Kafka returned to his writing with renewed vigor. In the early months of 1922, he wrote "The Hunger Artist," "Investigations of a Dog," "On Parables," and most importantly, he completed his longest, most ambitious project, *The Castle.* Later in the year, Kafka received approval of his request for early retirement from the Workers' Accident Insurance Institute, which allowed him to devote full days to his writing. As fate would dictate, however, Kafka's medical condition worsened in the months after his retirement. Forced to face his own mortality, Kafka asked his old friend, Max Brod, to promise to destroy his literary work upon his death.

KAFKA'S FINAL YEARS

In the final two years of his life, Kafka continued to write, producing his stories, "The Burrow," "A Little Woman," and "Josephine the Singer," his final work. He also experienced one last great love affair, with Dora Dymant, an Orthodox Jewish girl twenty years his junior. Kafka met Diamant on a trip to the Baltic coast in the summer of 1923.

In September 1923, Kafka moved fully out of his parents' apartment for the first time and into an apartment with Diamant in Berlin, where she was working for the Jewish People's Center. Owing to Kafka's meager pension and rampant inflation in Germany, the two lived in poverty. Kafka, however, said at the time that he was happier than he had ever been in his life.

Kafka's newfound happiness was short-lived. In March 1924, he was forced to return to his parents' apartment, where they could care for him during the progressing stages of his illness. Diagnosed with advanced tuberculosis of the larynx, he was soon admitted to a sanatorium near Vienna. He died with Diamant at his side on June 3, 1924, before the release of his short story collection, "The Hunger Artist." Kafka was buried in the Jewish cemetery in Prague on June 11. His father and mother were later buried in the same plot in 1931 and 1934, respectively, and his three sisters were later killed in Nazi concentration camps.

KAFKA'S LITERARY LEGACY

While Franz Kafka's life was cut short by illness, his friend, Max Brod, lived until 1968 and played an important role in keeping Kafka's literary legacy alive. In the last months of Kafka's life, Brod explains he saw Kafka truly happy, content with Diamant in Berlin, and working with pleasure on his final stories. When Brod suggested Kafka allow the publication of a collection of short stories, he took little convincing. "From all these circumstantial indications of his interest in life," Brod writes, "I then later gathered the courage to regard as no longer valid his written instructions to me—

written long before this period—which forbade the publication of any of his posthumous papers."[10]

Recognizing Kafka's talent and importance as a writer, Brod did not destroy his friend's work. Rather, Brod became Kafka's champion, editing most of his posthumous publications. Without Brod's efforts, literary scholars today might never have paid much attention to the few works published during Kafka's lifetime, like *The Metamorphosis*, which has become the most anthologized, most analyzed of his stories.

The Metamorphosis was one of the few stories Kafka wrote that he was not reluctant to publish, suggesting that it met with his exacting expectations of himself as a writer, despite the fact that he never quite approved of its ending. Critic Robert Gray describes *The Metamorphosis* as being unique among Kafka's other stories in its completeness and its lack of rambling and repetitiveness. It "shows all of the signs that Kafka was able to both portray his own situation and to achieve artistic mastery over it,"[11] Gray contends. With this story, Gray adds, Kafka had glimpsed his own life from the outside and gained, at the same time, a momentary escape from that life through his writing.

Walter Sokel agrees that *The Metamorphosis* can be read as a variation on Kafka's common theme—the inner, autobiographical life of the author. Gregor's transformation, for instance, represents Gregor's (and Kafka's) wish to abandon his responsibility for taking care of his family (Kafka was forced to work in the asbestos factory to help provide for his family), and, on another level, his desire to take revenge on his family's parasitic nature by feeding off them as a parasite himself (Kafka relied on his family to take care of him during his illness). However, Sokel reminds us, the images within *The Metamorphosis* work on a number of different levels, and "those who think that [Kafka's] protagonist's perspective is the whole of Kafka are victims of the subtle deception that this perspective perpetrates."[12]

Whether it is read for its autobiographical connections to Kafka or simply for its engaging story, *The Metamorphosis* is an appropriate introduction to the work of Franz Kafka. It is representative of the Czech writer's best work, offers insight into the feelings Kafka had about his own life, and holds a respected place in the archives of twentieth-century literature. Gray warns, however, that to fully understand Kafka, one must not study *The Metamorphosis* alone. Kafka was, Gray writes:

an extreme writer who abandoned himself to all the forces that could destroy a man, without trying to put in their way any of the conscious blocks that most of us use to separate ourselves from unacceptable insights. . . . His lasting quality will be found in a work that grows out of this basic integrity. But to see the work as a whole means taking into account more than individual passages. The patterns of whole stories and novels go towards making the full picture, and then too the pattern of Kafka's whole life as a writer has to be sought.[13]

NOTES

1. Quoted in Allan Blunden, "A Chronology of Kafka's Life," in *The World of Franz Kafka*. Ed. J.P. Stern. New York: Holt, Rinehart, and Winston, 1980, p. 12.
2. Max Brod, *Franz Kafka: A Biography*. New York: Schocken Books, 1963, p. 21.
3. Quoted in Brod, *Franz Kafka: A Biography*, p. 22.
4. Blunden, "A Chronology of Kafka's Life," p. 13.
5. Walter Sokel, "Franz Kafka," in *European Writers: The Twentieth Century*. Ed. George Stade. New York: Scribner, 1989, p. 1,151.
6. Brod, *Franz Kafka: A Biography*, p. 40.
7. Sokel, "Franz Kafka," p. 1,153.
8. Quoted in Brod, *Franz Kafka: A Biography*, p. 138.
9. Quoted in Gustav Janouch, *Conversations with Kafka*. New York: New Directions, 1971, p. 109.
10. Brod, *Franz Kafka: A Biography*, p. 198.
11. Ronald Gray, *Franz Kafka*. New York: Cambridge University Press, 1973, p. 84.
12. Sokel, "Franz Kafka," p. 1,160.
13. Gray, *Franz Kafka*, p. 28.

Characters and Plot

Characters

Gregor Samsa is a traveling salesman who awakens one morning to find himself transformed into a giant insect. Gregor becomes a burden to members of his family, who are forced to care for him in his new physical state. He thus suffers intense feelings of guilt over not being able to provide for them. Eventually rejected by his family and isolated from his capitalistic, industrial society, Gregor ultimately sacrifices his own well-being for the good of his family, starving himself and dying a death of alienation and loneliness.

Grete Samsa is Gregor's younger sister. She is the only one in the family with whom Gregor maintains any kind of intimacy after his transformation. She cleans his room and feeds him at the start, but she soon grows tired of her role as caregiver, leaving Gregor for longer periods of isolation. Although Gregor had generously planned to fund her violin studies at an expensive conservatory, Grete eventually suggests the family should dispose of Gregor after his metamorphosis.

Mr. Samsa, Gregor's father, allowed Gregor to support the family after his own business collapsed in failure. After Gregor's transformation, however, Mr. Samsa returns to work and gains a new vitality as the family provider once again. Suspicious and frightened of Gregor in his transformed state, Mr. Samsa forces him to remain in his room. He is also responsible for crippling Gregor by hurling an apple at him that remains painfully wedged in his back.

Mrs. Samsa, Gregor's mother, remains loving towards her son, but she is not very helpful to him as she often faints at the sight of him. She tries to protect Gregor from his father's anger and object throwing, but she does not have a lot of power within the family.

The Chief Clerk is Gregor's superior at work, who arrives at Gregor's apartment when he is late for work. The chief clerk is offended by Gregor's refusal to answer his bedroom door, and he humiliates Gregor when he says that he is suspected of stealing money from work. When the chief clerk sees Gregor's transformation, he flees from the apartment in horror.

Charwoman is the only family servant to stay on with the family after Gregor's change. Rather than being frightened by Gregor's transformation, she is intrigued by his new state and still sees in him some semblance of intelligence. She tries to play with Gregor, but he is intensely annoyed by her efforts.

The Three Lodgers rule over the Samsa household when they are taken in to supplement the family's income. The lodgers insist on order, inspect their food for inadequacies, and are disturbed by Grete's violin playing. When they see Gregor they give notice and refuse to pay for their time in the apartment. Mr. Samsa stands up to them, however, and they bow to his authority.

PLOT: PART 1

The novella begins as Gregor Samsa wakens from "uneasy dreams" to discover he has been transformed into a giant insect. He examines his new physique to find numerous thin legs, a hard shell for a back, and a soft, segmented belly. Seemingly unalarmed, Gregor remains calm and tries to return to sleep, but he is unable to get comfortable in his new physical state.

Gregor turns toward the clock and realizes that he is going to be late for his job as a traveling salesman. He dislikes getting up early for his job, his hard-nosed boss, irregular meals, and the fact that he is unable to make true friends on the road. He is unable to quit, however, because he is the provider for his family, which depends on his wages to survive. Having never missed a day's work in five years, Gregor believes it would be scandalous to call in sick. As he prepares to get out of bed, his mother calls for him outside his door. When he answers, he notices that his voice has changed along with his body. As the rest of the family realizes that Gregor has not yet left for work, they become concerned for his well-being. His father and sister join his mother at his locked door. In the meantime, Gregor has great difficulty in trying to get out of bed, as he is unable to move the lower part of his body without feeling considerable pain. He is forced to rock back and forth until he finally falls to the floor.

By 7:00 A.M., Gregor has made little progress in getting himself ready for work, and to make things more difficult for him, his boss, the chief clerk, arrives at his family's apartment to check up on him. Gregor is angry that his boss would come to his home when he is just barely late for work, and he refuses his father's request to open the door to allow the chief clerk to enter. Fearing that he will surely lose his job if his boss learns of his transformation, Gregor holds his ground even when the chief clerk loses his temper and proclaims that his behavior is disgraceful, his work of late has been unsatisfactory, and his position may be on the line.

While Grete, Gregor's sister, sobs in the next room, he tries to explain that he is simply indisposed and wishes to be left alone. His voice, however, has become unrecognizable, and his mother, fearing the worst, sends Grete to fetch the doctor, and her servant to fetch a locksmith. Gregor relaxes a little, relieved that his family is not in opposition to him, but rather, eager to help him. He next wedges himself against his door and is able to open the lock with his insect jaws. Upon witnessing Gregor's frightening transformation, the chief clerk backs quickly away. Gregor follows him into the hallway outside his room and begs him to understand his current plight and speak fairly of him at work so that he will not lose his job. In the meantime, Gregor's mother has fainted, and when she awakens, Gregor approaches her with snapping jaws, which further frightens her and gives the chief clerk an opportunity to escape the commotion in the apartment. Through clenched fists and tears, Gregor's father picks up a walking stick and waves it threateningly at Gregor to force him back into his room. When Gregor's awkward shell gets stuck in the doorframe, his father pushes him forcefully into the room from behind and slams the door closed.

PART 2

When Gregor awakens the next day, bruised from his father's aggressive treatment the day before, he finds that his sister has left food for him on the floor of his room. He is unable to drink the milk she has left, however. Feeling vulnerable in his position in the middle of the room, Gregor finds protection and solace under his sofa, and he remains there when his sister brings a variety of foods into his room. Soon, he discovers that he is only able to digest rotting cheese and vegetables. Grete is the only one who enters his room now, but the rest of the family, assuming that he cannot understand what they are saying, talks about him frequently and worries about the changes they are going to have to make in their lives to survive financially without his income. Gregor listens to their conversations through his closed door and learns that they are not eating as heartily as they used to. He begins to feel guilty and ashamed about the position he has left his family in, even though he learns his father has been hoarding some of Gregor's salary all along—enough that the family could have paid off their debts and Gregor could have quit his unrewarding job long ago.

As the days pass, Gregor takes part in few pleasurable activities. He enjoys looking out the window, but his eyesight has changed and he can no longer make out the shapes in the neighborhood. Out of boredom, he eventually begins to explore the floor and ceiling of his room so that he does not have to spend his days doing nothing at all. When his sister learns of these activities, she asks Mrs. Samsa to help her move Gregor's furniture out of his room so that he may have more room to explore. Gregor, however, agrees with his mother's assessment of the situation: His furniture is a link to his past, and if they remove it, it may be interpreted as a sign that they have given up on him.

In an effort to save something from his past life in his room, Gregor positions himself on his favorite picture, a woman wearing a fur, hanging on one of his walls. When his mother discovers him there, she faints. Grete exits the room to retrieve medicine for her mother, but she is startled to see that Gregor has followed her. She runs back to his room and slams the door shut, leaving him locked in the hall. When Gregor's father finds him there, he chases him and throws apples at him, painfully lodging one deep into his back, causing him to lose consciousness. At this point, his mother has been revived, and she pleads with Mr. Samsa to spare Gregor's life.

PART 3

After the escapade with the apples, Gregor's family leaves him largely neglected in his locked room. Due to his crippling injuries he finds it difficult to move around, and he can no longer gain any pleasure climbing the walls. After a short time, however, his father begins to feel sorry for him and allows his bedroom door to remain open so that he can watch his family together in the evenings. From his position under his sofa, Gregor notices how his family's lifestyle has changed in the short time since his metamorphosis. They have dismissed their maids (except for the charwoman), sold off their decorative ornaments, and look physically exhausted and despondent.

The more the family begins to focus on their own financial burdens, the less concerned they are about Gregor. He is hurt by his family's neglect and unamused by the charwoman, the only person in the household who pays him any kind of attention. Slowly, Gregor's room fills up with the family's discarded junk, and much of the family's furniture is stored in his room when they are forced to take in three lodgers to supplement their income. With the arrival of the lodgers, Gregor's door is now most often left closed. He grows depressed and eats less and less.

The lodgers begin to rule over the Samsa household, insisting on cleanliness and order. Mr. Samsa even bows to them upon returning home from work in the evening. One day the charwoman leaves Gregor's door ajar while the lodgers are in the living room, listening to Grete play the violin for them on request. The lodgers grow quickly bored with her performance, but Gregor is drawn towards the warmth of the music and has fantasies of convincing his sister to play for him in his room. When he ventures out of his room to be nearer Grete's playing, the lodgers stare at him, mystified and outraged that such a creature has been living secretly in the apartment. They announce that they cannot live in such squalid conditions, give notice, and refuse to pay the rent they already owe.

Grete responds to the scene by denouncing Gregor. She rejects that he is her brother, calls him a "creature," and demands that he be gotten rid of. If he were Gregor, she says, he would not stand by and let them live in these wretched conditions. Hearing Grete's outburst, Gregor feels her despair and longs for death. He slowly and painfully makes his way back to his room, remembering his family with thoughts of tenderness and love, and knowing that his death will release them from their current anguish. When Gregor finally makes it safely back to his room, Grete locks his door behind him.

In the morning, the charwoman announces Gregor's death, and the family takes some time to grieve for him in the Samsas' bedroom. Mr. Samsa then asks the lodgers to leave. At first they put up a fight, but they bow to his new forcefulness. The family then departs for a day in the country. The novella closes with images of their new vitality and hopes for the future: a smaller apartment, new and better jobs, and a husband for Grete, who has blossomed into a pretty girl, stretching herself in the sun.

CHAPTER 1

The Art of *The Metamorphosis*

Kafka's Artistic Achievement in *The Metamorphosis*

Ronald Gray

Ronald Gray is the University Lecturer in German at the University of Cambridge, and Fellow of Emmanuel College. His books include *Goethe the Alchemist*, *Kafka's Castle*, *Franz Kafka* and others. Although Kafka was unhappy with the ending of *The Metamorphosis*, Gray contends that the novella is one of the few works that Kafka was able to sustain through completion. The work exhibits a level of artistic achievement uncommon in Kafka's other works through its formal structure, its insistence on physical impossibility and presentation of paradoxical moods, and its comic relief, all of which afforded Kafka a brief escape from the unhappy circumstances of his own life.

'The Metamorphosis' (originally translated as 'The Transformation') took almost three weeks to write, from 18 November to 6 December, with interruptions on several evenings. For the first time, Kafka was able to hold a conception of some length and complexity over a period of weeks, and maintain its composition through to the end. This is the longest by far of all his completed works, and the only one in which the formal achievement is really important. Unlike any other of his stories, it is divided into three equal sections, each headed by a Roman numeral like an Act of a play, each section ending with a climactic moment. In the first, Gregor Samsa awakens to the realisation that he has turned into an insect and emerges from his bedroom, to be driven back by his infuriated father. In the second, he tries to accommodate himself to his absurdly hideous predicament, while his sister offers him various foods, doing all she can to reconcile herself and the family to

From *Franz Kafka*, by Ronald Gray. Copyright © 1973 by Cambridge University Press. Reprinted with the permission of Cambridge University Press.

the monster he has become; again, a brief sally into the living-room is repulsed by the father, this time even more violently, as he pelts Gregor with apples. In the third, Gregor comes out while his sister is playing the violin, entranced by the music which seems to be the 'food' he has so long been unable to find, but a third attack drives him back to die alone and untended. The family (excepting the father) having done all they can with their varying limitations, to acclimatise themselves, or to offer comfort and love, finally recognise their failure. After Gregor's death they turn with relief to the happier life that now awaits them.

Kafka was usually reluctant to have anything he had written published, and this remained true of 'The Metamorphosis': he declined Kurt Wolff's invitation to send it to him in April 1913, perhaps because Kafka intended it for a book planned long before, to be entitled 'Sons'. He did, however, send it in 1914 to the novelist Robert Musil, who accepted it for the *Neue Rundschau*, where it would have appeared but for opposition from the conservative management. And in the following year he came as near as he ever did come to urging a publisher to print a work of his, saying he was 'particularly concerned' to see publication. Considering Kafka's normal hesitancy, this suggests a strong feeling that the story came up to his expectations.

KAFKA'S ARTISTIC MASTERY

The formal excellence is striking enough in itself. Whereas very many of the stories are incomplete (including a large number of fragmentary beginnings in the diary, not normally printed in collections of the stories as such), or rambling and repetitive, 'The Metamorphosis' shows all the signs that Kafka was able both to portray his own situation and to achieve artistic mastery over it. That this is Kafka's situation, as he saw it, need not be doubted. He himself comments on the similarity between the name Samsa and his own. . . . The parents and the sister correspond closely to his view of his family, though only his sister Ottla seems to be included, and the sisters Elli and Vally are left out. It remains, of course, a projection from his own circumstances as much as any autobiographical subject in a novel does. The distinctive feature is the device by which Kafka omits all the repetitive doubts, the neurotic self-circlings, packing them all into the one image of the transformation, and viewing that as though from the outside. The transformation is at first sight incomprehensible, without some experience of it through Kafka's diaries. Yet it remains the obvious and most compelling image for his condition, as he saw it, and there is no symbolism about it, or rather the metaphorical element seems so slight, so ordinary, so much a matter of everyday speech that one scarcely wants to translate when Gregor discovers himself to be 'ein Ungeziefer' (a word which means 'vermin', rather than 'insect'). Gregor is, as one says, a louse. Nor does Kafka allow the comfort which might come from the expectation that the whole affair is a dream from which there will be an awakening. Exceptionally, there is no quality of dreams in this nightmare. Kafka insists on what the reader knows to be a physical impossibility, even though the general idea is common enough, because that is the only way that the full weight of his meaning can be conveyed, without overloading the story with the minutiae of self-recrimination. The conviction of being verminous is given full statement, once and for all, on the first page, and the rest becomes a matter of working out the practical details so that the truth comes home in concrete form.

This conviction is not the conviction of humanity at large, nor does the story ever make it out to be so; the implications exist for Gregor alone, and the rest of the characters are far from thinking themselves or being vermin. The notion that there is here what a recent school-edition described as 'an ultimately serious and universally human parable of man's fate' though obscurely conveyed in those words, seems to rest on a preconception that all men find themselves utterly repulsive, or should do. A not very different idea is expressed by another commentator, who finds here an exposure of the 'persistent primitiveness of man'. 'Shall we not say that the bug is better, more oneself', writes Paul Goodman, 'than the commercial traveller or the official in the insurance office?' and again, more emphatically, 'the animal-identity is deeper than the ordinary human being and his behaviour, it is nearer to the unknown deity. . . .' To deny this is not to remove all possible sympathy with Kafka's story, it is to maintain a sense of proportion. The cliché which says that every novelist worth his salt is normally describing Everyman is too persistent.

The really significant thing is the control which Kafka gains by stating his own condition, nobody else's, so simply. One of the principal advantages thus won is that, the interminable and inconclusive debates of later stories being excluded, he is able to take in the feelings and reactions of other people. The humanity which is lacking in some of the other stories, especially in 'In the Penal Colony', is more in evidence in 'The Metamorphosis'. The concentration on the *alter ego* who is the central character goes with a concentration on his relationship to the rest, simply because his condition is accepted without demur. What tenacity of will this acceptance implies needs little comment.

The whole story is worked out in terms of Gregor being an insect, and at no point does the reader have the sense of being slyly invited to see more than meets the eye. There are no enigmas in the dialogue, to be resolved (as in 'The Judgement') only by reference to Kafka's own life; though his life is latently present throughout, it is independent of the story and allows it to proceed without hindrance. At times in Kafka's writing he suggests compassion through some artificial device, as he does in 'A Hunger-Artist'. In 'The Metamorphosis' there are no devices, and the compassion is felt in the writing. It is not simply that the sister, confronted with an impossible situation, attempts the impossible in caring for the insect her brother has become, though the implications of that are moving in themselves. The love Gregor feels for her is in the rhythm of the prose, as when he hears her play the violin in the presence of the three lodgers. It is even more clearly present in the passage where Gregor's father starts throwing apples at him. The emotion mounts to a climax in which the urgency of the mother's pleading is as strongly present as the desperation of Gregor himself.

> The little red apples rolled around on the floor as though mag-netised, cannoning into one another. An apple thrown without much force grazed Gregor's back, but slid off without harm. Another, following immediately after it, however, sank deep into Gregor's back. Gregor tried to drag himself forward, as if the astounding, unbelievable pain might change if he moved to another place, but he felt as though he were nailed down, and flattened himself out in complete derangement of all his senses. The last thing he saw was the door of his room being flung open and his mother, followed by his shrieking sister, rushing in in her slip, as his sister had undressed her to let her breathe freely after her swoon, and then rushing up to his father, her petticoats falling down one after another, stumbling over the petticoats and hurling herself on his father, embracing him, in complete union with him—here Gregor's sight was already fail-ing—and with her hands clasped at the back of his father's head, pleading with him to spare Gregor's life.

PARADOXICAL MOODS

Strangest of all passages in Kafka, this has his double edge in
its most notable form. There is surely some human sympathy
here, in the portrayal of the mother, one wants to say, yet the
thought of Kafka's avowed detachment from the emotions his
readers were likely to feel, the calculating element in him, gives
cause for doubt. "An apple thrown without much force . . .'? It
sounds over-nonchalant when an insect is the target, and so
does the interest in the behaviour of the apples on the floor. Is
there a paradox present, or is the mood simply one of detachment? A touch of humour is noticeable even in the tragic situation. It is partly due to the petticoats falling down, partly something slightly stylised in the way the mother beseeches the
father—'beseeches' is the word, it has just that faint touch of the
melodramatic, and the mother's hands grasping the back of the
father's head also have a classic, and therefore stylised simplic-
ity. Certain overtones also appear, especially in the reference to
Gregor's being 'nailed down' and, differently, in the *coup de
grâce* of his seeing his mother and father perfectly united—the
one sight he would have preferred not to see—at the moment
that his eyesight dims. But above all there is the breathless rise
to a climax, grotesque in the circumstances when one realises
what kind of creature is being protected, and the urgency of
'Schonung' ('sparing'), uttered with the mother's own intensity.
Yet the whole is shot through with that mystical dissociation
that actually allows a humorous note to accompany every moment.

A similar paradoxical mood characterises the moment of
Gregor's death; not in itself, for the description here has nothing ironical or melodramatic, but in its context, in the events
which follow immediately on it. Left alone in his room with
the apple festering on him, he feels his strength ebb:

'And what now?' Gregor thought to himself, and looked round
in the darkness. He quickly discovered that he was unable to
move at all now. He was not surprised at that, it seemed unnatural to him that he should actually have been able to get about
up to this moment on these frail little legs. And on the whole he
did feel relatively comfortable. He had pains all over his body,
it was true, but he felt they were gradually becoming weaker
and weaker, and would in the end disappear completely. The
rotting apple in his back and the inflammation round it, covered with dirty fluff, scarcely troubled him. He thought again of
his family with affection and love. His feeling that he had to
vanish from the face of the earth was, if possible, stronger than

his sister's. In this state of vacant, peaceful contemplation he remained, until the tower clock struck three in the morning. He
was just conscious of the first brightening of the sky outside his
window. Then, without his willing it, his head sank to the floor,
and his last breath passed faintly through his nostrils.

There is no such moment as this anywhere else in Kafka, no
such calm recognition of what was a reality of his own condition. He is convinced here that Gregor must disappear from
the face of the earth, and the conviction has no resentment in
it, nor has it any expectation of Gregor's being rewarded by
some dialectical reversal of fortunes. Unlike Leverkühn in
Mann's *Doktor Faustus,* Gregor is not speculating on being a
particularly attractive morsel for divine. Grace to snap at; the
story is basically humanistic, atheistic, unconcerned about divine sanction or resurrection. Considering the savagery with
which 'In the Penal Colony' describes a death without prospect
of benefit, the calm of 'The Metamorphosis' is surprising. On
the other hand, it is not a passage to which one can do more
than assent. There is no other way out for Gregor, it is true, so
far as one can see from the story. Yet 'vacant, peaceful contemplation' is not particularly admirable, and the general sense is
of a feeble rather than a serene calm.

COMIC RELIEF

It is not a calm proudly presented for inspection. As soon as
Gregor's death has passed, Kafka allows the charwoman, one
of his best comic creations, to burst in. The reaction she shows
is inhuman if one still regards Gregor as a human being. But
that is the point: for the charwoman Gregor is not a human being; he is an insect and always has been. In allowing her to
show such indifference Kafka does, it is true, indicate that the
attempt of the sister at bridging the gap between herself and
Gregor is vain. The story has this utterly pessimistic note, so
far as Gregor is concerned, but the reader who finds this assertion of a human being's unloveableness unbearable may
have to see that it is also ineluctable. Gregor must vanish, and
the charwoman is chosen to say so:

> When the charwoman came, early in the morning,—out of
> sheer energy and impatience she slammed every single door,
> for all that she had been continually asked not to, so that from
> the moment she arrived there was no possibility of sleeping
> anywhere in the whole flat—she at first found nothing spe-
> cial in her first customary, cursory visit to Gregor. She
> thought he was lying so motionless on purpose, playing at be-

ing insulted; she credited him with every conceivable kind of intelligence. Happening to have the long broom in her hand, she tried tickling Gregor from the door. Obtaining no success that way either, she became annoyed and shoved at Gregor a little, and only when she had pushed him from where he lay without the least resistance did she begin to take notice. Quickly seeing how things stood, she opened her eyes wide, whistled to herself, but did not take long before she had flung open the door of the bedroom and shouted into the darkness at the top of her voice, 'Come and have a look, it's done for, lying there done for it is!'

Kafka could only have written in that way out of an inner certainty which recognised the crude life of the charwoman as decidedly as he recognised his own nature, or the dominant aspect of his own nature. The charwoman sweeps back into the scene like something out of a comic postcard, a self-sufficient bull of a woman, although as she does so, a critical reservation in Kafka's mind begins to make itself felt. . . . Gregor is dead, but the victory is not with the opposition. There is a certain comedy already in the slight hesitation shown by the charwoman about opening such a thing as a bedroom-door early in the morning, and this now develops into a further not wholly serious situation, as Herr and Frau Samsa, woken by her shouting, get out of bed symmetrically. This is kept up in the description of the three lodgers—a main source of comedy in the story—who act with the perfect uniformity of the decent, convention-respecting man. They take their hats from the hat-stand, their sticks from the umbrella-stand, all at the same moment, they bow, and go down the stairs; reappearing at regular intervals as the landings hide them or bring them into view. One sees here Kafka's ironical reserve, working from a point of view well behind the horrifying persona with which he had to live. . . .

This is still not the end of Kafka's comment; amusing as these moments are (if one can see them from out of his wretched state), they offer more light relief than social criticism. . . . There remains the final scene when, Gregor being dead, the family is at last free of him and decides, since it is springtime, to take a tram-ride for an excursion into the country. The last sentences have some of Kafka's best cadences as well as his fullest vision:

> While they were conversing like this, it occurred almost at the same moment to Herr and Frau Samsa, seeing their daughter's vitality return more and more strongly, that despite the sorrow which had brought a pallor to her cheeks she had recently blossomed into a pretty girl with an attractive figure.

Falling silent, and almost unconsciously exchanging understanding glances, they reflected that it would soon be time to be
finding a proper young man for her. And it was like a confirmation of their fresh dreams and good intentions when, as they
arrived at the end of their journey, their daughter rose to her
feet first and stretched her young body.

A Brief Escape from the Self

[This is Kafka most fully in possession of himself as a writer.
The verminous self must go: it has no hold on life, and no des-
tiny but extinction.] On the other hand, the brave new world
now emerges, not unsatirised: the parents are still slightly uniform and symmetrical, and such good intentions as they may
have are coloured by the half-conscious, and presumably calculating glances they exchange, their minds half-fixed on what
advantages a suitor may bring. But the story does end with that
glimpse of a woman ready for love and marriage; there are sub-
tleties and simplicities here of a human order.

The ending was the one part of the story Kafka could not approve. At the moment he finished it he wrote to Felice to tell her
so, adding, 'only the ending as it is today doesn't make me feel
glad, it could have been better, there's no doubt.' Whether he
had anything specific in mind is impossible to say; he very sel-
dom did make specific criticisms of his work. Not much more
than a year later, he again rejected the ending, and perhaps the
whole story with it: 'Great dislike of "Metamorphosis". Unreadable ending. Imperfect almost to the very bottom. It would have
been better if I had not been disturbed by the business trip.' Unlike his objections to *America*, this did not prevent him from trying to get the story published. Did he dislike the momentary
suggestion of an optimistic conclusion with its possible insin-
cerity (as it probably was, for him)? What he had written was,
all the same, more subtle than mere optimism would have been.
And it was in any case a very brief escape. In 'The Metamorphosis' he had seen his own existence as though from outside,
in its relation with other lives, and though there was always another self which watched this self, he had recognised the need
for this self to die. It was a personal affair, and he made no more
of it than that, in this story. Had he realised the implications, he
might never have written in the same vein again.

Within a short while, however, the conviction that his own
state could represent a universal fact of existence entered his
consciousness, and the stories he wrote after this are given a
more general symbolic value.

The Impersonal Narrator of *The Metamorphosis*

Roy Pascal

Roy Pascal is a distinguished scholar of the narrative art of European novelists and autobiographers. His book *Kafka's Narrators: A Study of His Stories and Sketches* is considered a groundbreaking study, providing a new appreciation of Kafka's work. Pascal defines the narrator of *The Metamorphosis* as an impersonal, or non-personal, one. While the supreme function of narrators in fiction is to communicate the main character's view and judgment of the world, the narrator of *The Metamorphosis* acts more as an independent, technical aid to the narrative. It is the narrator's seeming objectivity to the events at hand that invites readers to enter Kafka's world of imagination and to ultimately suspend their disbelief.

For 'The Metamorphosis', Kafka adopted a non-personal narrator, and its first sentence proclaims the subordination of the narrator to the chief character. 'When Gregor Samsa awoke one morning out of restless dreams he found himself in his bed transformed into a monstrous bug.' From this moment the narrator identifies himself almost completely with Gregor, sees and hears through his eyes and ears, and accepts the truth of his metamorphosis as the victim himself must. Except in the coda of the last few pages, describing the revival of the family after the death of Gregor, almost everything we know is passed on to us via the consciousness of Gregor. To his thoughts we have direct access, the others we know as Gregor sees them through the open door and overhears their conversation. His thoughts and impressions are sometimes reported by the narrator much like his spoken words, in inverted commas introduced by such

From *Kafka's Narrators: A Study of His Stories and Sketches*, by Roy Pascal. Copyright © 1982 by Cambridge University Press. Reprinted with the permission of Cambridge University Press.

verbs as 'thought'. But they also invade many passages which, while seeming to express a narrator's view, betray the personal source by a characteristic word here or there. For instance, in the first paragraph, the last sentence might be read as a narrator's comment: 'His many—in relationship to his bulk pitifully thin—legs waved helplessly before his eyes.' But the preceding sentences have described what Gregor could see of his body when he raised his head, and we are meant to feel the 'pitifully' is *his* thought as much as the 'waved' applies to *his* vision.

The text continues:

> 'What has happened to me?' he thought. It was no dream. His room, a proper human room—albeit a little too small—lay calmly between its four familiar walls. Above the table on which a collection of materials had been spread out—Samsa was a commercial traveller—hung the picture which he had recently cut out of an illustrated magazine and mounted in a pretty gilt frame.

The first sentence in inverted commas seems to distinguish Gregor's thoughts from the 'facts' the narrator lists. But this distinction does not hold. 'It was no dream' is evidently a conclusion of Gregor's, not the narrator's, since the normal appearance of his room proves it. Not merely 'calmly' has meaning only if thought by Gregor, also the odd phrase, 'a human room—albeit a little too small', critical and reassuring together, has meaning only if it is a rumination of Gregor's, showing the mean, carping spirit in his smugness. Other items in the room, his samples and the picture, are mentioned as his eyes travel to them, and again the expression 'pretty gilt frame' with its smugness has meaning only if it belongs to him and not the narrator. But, on the other hand, the parenthesis 'Samsa was a commercial traveller' is an explanatory communication from narrator to reader.

THE NARRATOR'S INDEPENDENT FUNCTION

This narratorial passage is followed by Gregor's resentful reflexions on his unsatisfactory profession and his superiors, given in direct speech; a long passage of free indirect speech, peppered with exclamatory questions and characteristic phrases (as when the porter is called 'the boss's minion, a creature with no backbone or mind of his own'); narratorial descriptions of his behaviour as he tries to get out of bed, listens to what his family is doing or saying when the chief clerk (*Prokurist*) arrives etc.; and reproductions of the discussions Gregor hears, and takes part in, given in direct speech. None of these methods provides problems of interpretation except the narratorial descriptive form, which consistently betrays that ambiguity we have already observed in the opening two paragraphs. That is: while the narrator's standpoint is determined by the consciousness and concern of the character Gregor and he usually is concerned only to make Gregor's feelings and intentions evident, he also sometimes demonstrates a more independent purpose and indeed offers the reader the chance of becoming the objective observer he emphatically does become in the final pages, after Gregor's death. It is this narratorial stance that requires a closer examination, the object of which can be formulated thus: why, if the supreme function of the narrator is to communicate to the reader the chief character's view and judgment and his world, without the corrective of an authoritative evaluation, does this narrator still retain some independence of function? This independence appears in several forms.

The chief form is as a technical aid to the narrative. This we have already seen when the parenthesis 'Samsa was a commercial traveller' enables us to understand why Gregor's eye lights on certain objects in his room. There are many such bits of helpful information that the narrator smuggles in, as if, when we are looking at a detective film, a neighbour who has already seen it whispers to us what we should look out for. In this way we are told that the Samsa's maid keeps to the kitchen and locks the door, we receive a precise description of the elaborate meal that Gregor's sister puts out for him, and brief character-sketches of the new charwoman and the trio of lodgers. It is true that often there are suggestions that these facts are present to Gregor's consciousness, as when the information that all three lodgers have beards is, as it were, validated by the statement 'as Gregor once noticed through the crack of the door' but it is clear that our information often comes from some other source than Gregor. I do not think these occasional bits of supplementary information weaken in any way the intensity of the narrative, since they do not offer an alternative view or evaluation.

It is different with one such addition. The scene when Gregor intrudes into the family room, in which his sister is playing to the lodgers, is in all essentials described from his point of view, perhaps with a few enlargements to compensate for the limitations imposed on his vision. But as he creeps into the full sight of the lodgers and the family and creates panic among them, we are told of the filthy state he is in, with 'threads, hair, remains of food' clinging to his back. For a moment we see him as the others see him, in a state he is unconscious of (normally he is only too aware of his disgusting appearance). This constitutes a change of perspective that is different from the others mentioned, since it means a switch from the main character's consciousness to that of other characters, and though it is only a momentary effect, I find it disconcerting. That we feel it as a dislocation must be due to the depth of our normal absorption in the perspective of the chief character. For, from the first sentence, it is Gregor himself who sees himself changed into a loathsome bug, while the others (including the narrator) only confirm what he feels and asserts. It is only under this condition that the story—fairy-tale or parable—is presented to us.

There are also other ways in which the narrator's hand is evident, especially when the story is temporarily released from the account of concrete events as they occur in Gregor's presence. Occasionally the narrator summarizes a process, telling us for instance 'In this way Gregor was given his food every day' or 'Gregor spent the days and nights with almost no sleep'. The long account of his labors for his family and his hopes to retrieve his father's business failure and provide for the education of his sister is expressly stated to represent the 'utterly useless thoughts' running through his head while he listens to the family discussion, but the succinct narratorial account here again puts the reader at a distance from the situation, frees him from the immediacy of the tale, gives him the relief of an intellectual grasp of the situation. The most striking passage of this kind is the opening of the third section of the story. Here the narrator sums up the change in the father's attitude to Gregor during the month that followed his father's furious attack on him. Now, we are told, the father seemed to have decided to treat him as a member of the family, not an enemy; and we understand that Gregor gathers this from various bits of evidence available through the open sitting-room door. We can even hear a typical bit of complex free indirect speech in the last words of this paragraph, that 'family duty commanded that one swallowed one's disgust and suffered, accepted and suffered', for it is Gregor's thought quoting unmistakably the overheard words of his father. Here again, though we cannot speak of a different perspectival angle in these words, since their source is as ever the character Gregor Samsa, there is the difference of distance, a distance in this case peculiar to story-making, a long temporal focus replacing the near focus and thus inducing a relaxation of the almost unbearable tension of the story. For this tension arises not simply from the horror of the events but above all from our inescapable immersion in them through the nature of the narrative perspective.

A SUSPENSION OF DISBELIEF

Such pauses in the movement of a narrative are very common in traditional novels and function as a temporary relaxation of tension. . . . They belong naturally to a type of narrative structure in which the intrusive authoritative narrator has many such tricks at his disposal. But, while in 'The Metamorphosis' such changes in the temporal or spatial perspective are few and slight, they achieve a relaxation of a different type, one that affects not the tension of a dramatic event but the whole oppressive spell the reader submits to as a result of the narrative perspective. These slight pauses are indeed anticipations of the change that occurs after Gregor's death, when the family revives, decently rejoicing in its liberation from the son who, while he was their chief support, had because of this drained them of responsibility and confidence. The reader too, now freed from the mediation of Gregor, has direct access to their thoughts and feelings, even to those of the charwoman. So that this coda seems in fact to be outside the magic circle of the story. Kafka twice expressed his distaste for this 'unreadable ending', but gave no hint of the grounds for his dissatisfaction.

Different readers will feel these variations in the narrative perspective with different intensity. But all would agree that, if there is any inconsistency in the structure, it impairs hardly at all the power of the work. If we have in part answered the questions posed above, we have still to face the most important, underlying question: why does Kafka employ in these tales an impersonal narrator, if his essential function is only to communicate the chief character's view? Why should he not have written a first-person story and avoided the lapses that have been pointed out? The question has relevance in regard to other Kafka stories too, and in particular to the novels.

In the first place, the use of such a narrator is a great technical convenience, since it makes it possible to establish a physical scene or sum up a long process with greater clarity and economy than if the author is closely bound to the consciousness of the character. Though the narrator stands beside the character and remains true to his perspective, he can select and order the objects or events in the character's experience in order to make the appropriate impact on the reader. Every character, like every living person, registers his outer and inner experience with differing grades of awareness, and at any particular moment will not always be able to distinguish the significant from the trivial; the narrator can so differentiate and by various means can subtly make the reader aware of a line of significance within a chaos of contingency—as for instance he does at the opening of the story, when Gregor responds to his appalling transformation with the apparently ludicrously irrelevant and trivial resentment directed at his employers.

Of course, in stories of the type of 'The Judgment' and 'The Metamorphosis', in which the chief character dies, an external narrator is particularly useful, not simply because the character cannot describe his own death and its results, but also because it is hard to find for a dead man the perspective in which he would see his past life. There are in fact stories written in the first person in which this person dies, but the endings always seem awkward and contrived. We shall find that in his later stories Kafka repeatedly prefers a first-person narrative, but for stories which describe a continuing situation which lacks a conclusive ending.

The interpretative function of the objective impersonal narrator in both these early Kafka stories is, above all, the provision of a guarantee for the events recounted, a guarantee of a special kind. The objective voice seems to confirm the character's situation through an impersonal affirmation and a slightly different focus, slightly further away from things than the character himself. We can detect its general effect in that startling first sentence of 'The Metamorphosis': 'When Gregor Samsa awoke one morning out of restless dreams he found himself in his bed transformed into a monstrous bug.' Though we later discover that this statement corresponds to Gregor's own conviction, it is in its form deliberately and emphatically an objective narratorial assertion and this fact should not be wiped out of the reader's consciousness. We hear in it the objective voice of fiction, the invitation to enter the world of imagination and to suspend disbelief. Because of the authoritative nature of this narratorial voice, that makes itself heard from time to time later in the story, we are warned against taking the story as the mere account of a character's hallucination or as a study in psychopathology. But what guarantee does this voice give? This calm constatation [sic] of a fantastic monstrosity is clearly not intended to persuade us that it and the following events belong to the normal order of reality, however realistic, psychologically and physically, their description may be. How then do we read it? I believe as a folk-tale or parable in which, if we are presented with unrealistic fantasies, we know that we are not thereby invited to take them as real in an ordinary sense but urged to look into them for some meaning, some illumination on life that they will provide through their impact upon the circumstances into which they burst. The guarantee of the impersonal narrator is a guarantee of meaning; he asks us to accept the presupposition of Gregor's metamorphosis in order (as we find out) to enquire into the relations of son and father, son and family, and especially the power-rivalries involved—in the same way as in Kafka's novels, *The Trial* and *The Castle*, we are not to question the reality and authority of the law courts or the castle but to experience the meaning they have for the characters who seek admittance. This is a typical feature of Kafka's story-telling that . . . forces the reader to look beyond the surface network of the story for another, symbolic meaning.

A PRESENTNESS OF EXPERIENCE

But if we now consider together these various items that the impersonal narrator contributes to 'The Metamorphosis', we find this contribution is of greater significance than we earlier suspected. For, taken together, they establish the structure of a story—not only are the scenes filled out by pieces of narratorial information, but the narrator opens and closes the story, sets the scenes, establishes them as phases of a story for which he also determines the movement in time, allowing us sometimes to be absorbed in the moment, sometimes from a longer focus to view the passage of days. In 'The Metamorphosis', as could be observed in 'The Judgment', the narrator's adoption of the main character's perspective makes the reader experience the events as if they were present, especially in the sense that they have the incoherence of the present and do not point to an outcome. But this presentness of experience is conveyed through the past tense, the narrative preterite, with which both stories open and continue. And, from the beginning of each story, this past tense proclaims that we are to read events that make up a completed whole, that is told, as it were, in retrospect. Because of this, the story can be articulated in its structure, have its phases that lead to its outcome. Thus a double process takes place in the reader. On the one hand he is immersed in the experience of the main character, cut off from an alternative source and alternative evaluations; but on the other hand he is directed by the structure of the story, which is cunningly devised both to provide an intense participation in the character's experience but also to establish it as forming a whole with a peculiar coherence. In this way the Kafka narrator provides therefore not only for experience but also for understanding; for understanding is the *raison d'être* of story-telling, even if the understanding implied is not what we usually expect by the term. . . . 'The whole seems meaningless, it is true, but is in its peculiar way complete.' The 'meaning' Kafka refers to here is not any allegorical message, but more simply the use or function of the various parts of the figure, their relationship to one another, their coherence. . . . The reader is at first troubled to grasp the psychological coherence of the various parts, the connection of event and mental response, of purpose and behavior, of words and thoughts. But the story structure, its completeness, forces us to seek this coherence, to discover relationships between thoughts and situations, the coherence of this apparent incoherence, to accept in fact a coherence that is startlingly different from that which the conventional story has lived by.

Gregor Samsa
Is a Parasite

Thomas F. Barry

Thomas F. Barry is a professor in the Department of German at the University of Southern California, Los Angeles. Barry defines Gregor Samsa's transformation in *The Metamorphosis* as one of the most innovative uses of metaphor in modern literature. In his own life, Kafka felt much like a parasite, living off his father and others after being diagnosed with tuberculosis. Similarly, Samsa relies on his family for sustenance after his horrific transformation. He becomes, in fact, a parasitic vampire, aggressively yet unconsciously feeding off his loved ones until he is shunned by them completely and ultimately sacrificed for the greater good of all.

Kafka's story "The Metamorphosis," written during the months of November and December 1912 and published in 1915, undoubtedly remains the best known of the author's compositions and has generated a considerable amount of critical attention. The most striking element in the text is Gregor Samsa's bizarre transformation, a metamorphosis of man into insect involving one of the most innovative uses of metaphor in modern literature. . . .

ON PARASITES AND METAPHORS

Kafka's language, his imagery and metaphors, is an artful catalogue of symptoms, condensations (*Verdichtungen*) of psychic trauma, pairings of arrested signifiers that feed off other signifieds and off the body of public discourse. Kafka the parasite artist exploited the symptoms of Kafka the man, nourished his art with the blood of his life and that of others, above all of his father and of women. One thinks of the diary entry of September 12, 1917 when Kafka first learned that he had tuberculosis; his illness became for him a symbol of his inner

From "On the Parasite Metaphor in Kafka's *Metamorphosis*," by Thomas F. Barry, *West Virginia University Philological Paper*, vol. 35, 1989. Reprinted with permission from the author.

spiritual illness, of his relationships to Felice Bauer and to his father. Like a parasite—the primary etymology of which, *parasitos* or "beside the grain," suggests a guest at a meal, especially a professional dinner guest who never returns an invitation—the writer lived alongside his host, taking the food of his art but never or rarely giving anything in return. Kafka, we know, did not publish much of his work during his lifetime, and at his death he wanted the rest destroyed. For various reasons, he did not want to share what he had taken.

As J. Hillis Miller indicates in his essay on deconstructionist readings of literature, the word parasite is particularly rich in etymological associations that imply paradox and the simultaneity of opposites. The word is itself a shifting play of signifiers that seem to evoke and cancel each other. The parasitical implies the paradoxical because by seeking its food, the parasite ultimately destroys its host and often thereby itself. The word suggests a relationship of proximity and distance, similarity and difference and contains further associations of both guest and host, alien invader and friendly presence, sacrificial victim and sacrificing master, a benevolent or malevolent ghost. The parasite is the alien Other within the self. Kafka's texts portray the parasite that lives off others, literally in works such as "The Metamorphosis" and "Jackals and Arabs," and even the early story "Wedding Preparations in the Country.". . .

The most obvious image of the parasite in Kafka's works is, of course, in "The Metamorphosis," the best known of his texts. Although Kafka did not use the sign "Parasit" but instead the term "Ungeziefer" in reference to his character, the words are equivalent and the conceptual associations are the same. The Greek prefix "para-" suggests, among other meanings, the notion of incorrectly resembling something else as well as wrongfully or harmfully existing beside. This is as good a description as any of Gregor Samsa, the insect parasite that incorrectly resembles a human being and that wrongfully and harmfully lives next to his family. With the consciousness of a man and the body of a vermin, he is grotesque, a monstrosity that threatens the well-being of all. His metamorphosis becomes, as Gunther Anders and Walter Sokel suggest, a literal enactment of metaphor. If Freud's first patients were afflicted with the metaphoric symptoms of hysterical paralysis or physical arrest . . . as the result of sexual trauma or psychological arrest . . . then Gregor's physical transformation too is an outward metaphoric symptom/sign of an internal conflict that cannot find direct expression. . . .

The idea of a parasite implies by definition that of a host (and with host that of both guest and ghost), and in the figure of Gregor all of these associations are active. He is a traveling salesman, more often a guest within his own family and like a guest in a strange hotel, he locks his door at night (as did Kafka in his parents' apartment): "He felt thankful for the prudent habit he had acquired in traveling of locking all doors during the night, even at home". The locked door also suggests that he is an alien presence, an invading host or army within the friendly territory of his family, something from which they must be protected. Although Gregor initially serves as the provider-host of his parents and sister, he becomes (again paradoxically) the ghost that haunts his family, the guest/ghost that must be locked away. There is a repressed violence and aggression towards his family in Gregor that must be contained. He is the ultimate supernatural ghost parasite—the vampire—who begins to drain his family of its strength. As there is in the sexualized feeding of the vampire, there is, as we shall see, a strong erotic component in the parasite image in Kafka.

Curiously, Gregor is not the typical guest implied in the word parasite—one who eats the host's food but never returns any—because he does not even partake of his family's provisions, at least the material ones. After his transformation, his sister Grete begins to bring him the rotten leftovers of the others' meal but later he cannot even eat these. The issue of food and hunger is central to "The Metamorphosis" (and other Kafka texts as well) as it is to the parasite, and we might well look here for insight into Gregor's parasitical nature. Gregor's appetite makes him long for the unknown food ("die unbekannte Nahrung") and it is ultimately a psychic sustenance that he seeks. We find an indication of what this food is near the end of the story when the sister plays the violin for the renters. Gregor is drawn to the music and feels that this is the unknown nourishment that he has been seeking: "He felt as if the way were opening before him to the unknown nourishment he craved". We know that Kafka was himself drawn to Schopenhauer's *The World as Will and Idea* in which music and art are central concepts. Music is the most perfect art form because it replicates the Will (the undifferentiated life force) most closely. . . .

THE PARASITE VAMPIRE

The scene with the music is linked to Gregor's erotic phantasy with his sister, whom he will lock away in his room so that he alone may possess her. Since the parasite seeks to merge with its host in the sexualized act of feeding and yet in so doing destroys itself (or at the very least its life-sustaining source of food), it serves as a perfect representation of the erotic death that motivates Gregor and, we presume, his author: Kafka the paradoxical parasite who existed in paragraphs and parables as a means of displacing himself (the "para-" prefix again meaning "beside" or "next to"). It is not food or money that Gregor seeks from his family, but, like a vampire, he wants the blood of their psychic-erotic energy. The image of the parasite is one of aggressive sexuality; it achieves union with the host through the act of destroying it: a vampire *Liebestod*. The parasite incorporates the union of eros and thanatos in a single signifier; it is both the eater and the eaten. The sexualized vampire parasite is quite obvious in Gregor's phantasy with his sister/host Grete in which he, the insect, falls upon her neck in a grotesque attempt at union: "and Gregor would then raise himself to her shoulder and kiss her on the neck, which, now that she went to business, she kept free of any ribbon or collar". Women are the primary hosts in Kafka's stories and it is Grete who—in another paradoxical reversal of terms—ultimately rejects Gregor from the family. She becomes the doctor who diagnoses the family's illness as its parasite son. In the well-known passage at the end of the second section, it is clear that he also seeks erotic union with the mother/host, though as with the sister, this too is thwarted.

Before his transformation, Gregor was the host who supported his parasitical family, especially his father, who spent his days dozing in his chair while his son worked his impossible job as a salesman. This situation is, of course, reversed as Gregor becomes the parasite and the family his unwilling host. Such reversals of terms are, we remember, characteristic of the word parasite and its etymology; the guest suddenly becomes the invader, the sacrificial victim the one who performs the sacrifice. Gregor is now transformed into the host/victim (the German "Ungeziefer" from the Hebrew suggesting this) and Kafka seems to intend the religious associations of the word host for, in Gregor's eventual sacrifice, the family is redeemed. The parasite vampire who exploits becomes the Christ figure who saves. . . .

In nature the parasite-host relationship is one of power and struggle as the host organism attempts to reject the invader, sometimes successfully and sometimes not. This is certainly the case with the father/host who battles with the son/parasite. The father (and the chief clerk) represent the forces of the body/society—its immunity—that confront the alien interloper and the sickness it carries with the standards of health and well-being. The figure of the father and the "vital" truths of marriage/family/bourgeois profession that he symbolizes for Kafka rise against the son and condemn him . . . for the parasite aggression he unconsciously directs towards the family. When Gregor, with insect jaws snapping, approaches his mother, it is the father who preserves the immunity of the others against the disease of the son.

Images of Doors Provide Meaning in *The Metamorphosis*

Leonard Moss

Leonard Moss has published in *Modern Philology* and *Educational Theatre Journal.* He is Associate Professor of English at the State University of New York in Genesco. Moss explores images of doors in *The Metamorphosis.* For Gregor, there is virtually no existence in the life beyond his room, his cramped sense of self, and the confines of his family. Therefore doors, and especially the door to Gregor's room, represent alternately both a cell his family locks him within, and a means for security and retreat. Ironically, while doors create distance between characters in *The Metamorphosis*, blocking opportunities for communication and intimacy, it is only through confinement that Gregor is able to relate to his family.

The action of "The Metamorphosis" may be seen as a series of approaches and withdrawals occurring in the problematic relationship between Gregor Samsa and his family, particularly his father. Each side at times desires to achieve communication with the other, yet every movement toward rapport is blocked by an undefined, impassable obstacle, until at last the relationship deteriorates so radically that only the death of Gregor can release his family and himself from intolerable frustration. Resolution through death, after the change from tolerance to disgust, denial, and alienation, concludes the story's spiritual progression. Kafka has made this progression concrete by his constant allusion to doors, the work's most important image after the insect analogy. Open, a door may admit a person to intimacy with another; locked, it keeps others from one's private world. Through almost one hundred refer-

From "A Key to the Door Image in *The Metamorphosis*," by Leonard Moss, *Modern Fiction Studies*, vol. 17, no. 1 (1971), pp. 37–42. Copyright © Purdue Research Foundation. Reprinted by permission of the Johns Hopkins University Press.

ences to the open or closed doors surrounding Gregor, Kafka constructs a situation in which a character is figuratively as well as literally closed off from life because of his own inability, and the inability of those closest to him, to penetrate the wall of misunderstanding and resentment separating them.

The story as a whole, then, represents successive degrees of withdrawal in an overall decline; at the same time, each of the three sections is itself a miniature version of the central movement from tolerance to antipathy. At the beginning of the first section the prospect of rescue is keenest. A "cautious tap" at the door between Gregor's and his parents' bedrooms accompanies the mother's "gentle voice" expressing concern for her late-rising son. Across the room Gregor's sister takes up the attempt to reach the indisposed young man through *her* closed bedroom door, whereupon the father, at still another door to Gregor's bedroom (this opens to the living room), introduces the first discordant voice. Undeterred by any thought that his son might be in serious trouble or perhaps incapacitated, the elder Samsa assumes Gregor to be morally delinquent in wilfully refusing to attend to his job, which supports the family. Selfishly, he seeks his son's absence, not proximity, when he knocks at the door "gently, yet with his fist." All three overtures to Gregor, whether gentle or insistent, fail to impel him to remove the barrier. Motivated by dismay at his own monstrous appearance (rather than by hostility at the intrusiveness of the others), he refuses to admit them into his room: "He was not thinking of opening the door, and felt thankful for the prudent habit he had acquired in traveling of locking all doors during the night, even at home."

Though he requires assistance to leave his room, Gregor persistently rejects the idea of enlisting support because of his paralyzing sense of worthlessness; his contempt for himself finds an adequate image, of course, in the repulsive shape and "horrible twittering" of a roach. Fearing the "anxiety, if not terror" that his presence will cause "behind all the doors," he at first refuses to leave his sanctuary, then realizes that if he were to "take the risk" of opening the door he would need "help" from "two strong people"—such as his father and the servant girl. Meanwhile the pressure exerted on him to reenter the family area intensifies upon the entrance (through the outside door to the apartment) of Gregor's superior, the chief clerk. As before, Gregor is pummeled by voices passing through the three surrounding locked doors, urging that he rejoin the family and resume his position in the world. As before, Gregor, who except for his job does not dwell much in that world—in the preceding eight days he "has stayed at home every single evening"—refuses to unlock the door. He continues, typically, to feel shame at his own repulsiveness rather than anger at the clerk's insolence.

A RETREAT BEHIND DOORS

By the time Gregor does resolve "to open the door," his father has sent for additional "help" to extricate him from his seclusion—a doctor and a locksmith. These two outsiders, substituting for the father and servant as potential rescuers, are called to minister to the presumed malfunctions of man and door. Congruence between the two problems becomes clear once Gregor's physical predicament is taken to symbolize his spiritual predicament: "He felt himself drawn once more into the human circle and hoped for great and remarkable results from both the doctor and the locksmith, without really distinguishing precisely between them." But finding it even less conceivable to relate to foreign benefactors than to accept family helpers, he determines again to unlock the door to his cell without aid. Ironically, the only one to offer encouragement during the slow turning of the key is the clerk, another outsider ("they should all have shouted encouragement to him," Gregor laments, "his father and mother too").

Although Gregor succeeds in opening the bedroom door ("so I didn't need the locksmith"), he has little hope that any good will result; indeed, his re-emergence, as he feared, antagonizes everyone, especially his father, who clenches his fist for the second time "as if he meant to knock Gregor back into his room." Gregor does not in fact enter the living room immediately; instead, he remains leaning against the *inside* of the door, looking out his bedroom window and through the open hall and front doors. Neither a window nor an outside door, however, provides an exit from the confrontation that for him must take place in a family context. Once the ordeal begins, he considers his sister his only ally, but her intelligence and sympathy cannot alleviate his problem. "She would have shut the door of the flat" against the intrusion of the chief clerk, he muses, "and in the hall talked him out of his horror. But she was not there, and Gregor would have to handle the situation himself." Gregor does *not* handle the situation: his mother and the clerk recoil in revulsion, his father wishes to "drive Gregor back" past the door he had laboriously opened. His contortions in trying first to approach, then to escape the gathering are ludicrous, pitiable, revolting. Finally, wounded (and "bleeding freely") by the treatment of those he loves, he retreats behind his three closed doors to the "deliverance" from rejection that he discovers in "silence."

The second section of "The Metamorphosis" begins and ends in a similar way: the family's tentative tolerance gives place to aversion, until for the second time Gregor is driven back through the door of his room, mortally wounded now by a father who will not accept this detestable vermin as a son. In this section the expectation that Gregor might be reintegrated with his family becomes markedly diminished. True, he is permitted to exist, but now there are no overtures to rejoin the group: "Gregor now stationed himself immediately before the living room door, determined to persuade any hesitating visitor to come in or at least to discover who it might be; but the door was not opened again and he waited in vain." This absence of direct contact reduces him to eavesdropping through the locked doors. Occasionally he gazes out the window, "obviously in some recollection of the sense of freedom that looking out of a window always used to give him," but soon he curtails this pastime too. The servant "keeps the kitchen door locked," and even Grete "slammed the [bedroom] door shut again." Later she "jumped back as if in alarm and banged the door shut; . . . this made him realize how repulsive the sight of him still was to her." Grete leaves food scraps for Gregor, yet because he can find no nourishment in those remnants his body slowly dries up.

Thus the principal character withdraws into the deepening isolation of his own room—"a room where Gregor lorded it all alone over empty walls." At one point, on seeing his furniture ("everything he loved") being removed, indignation compels him to rush past the door, but as usual his intentions are misunderstood and he is, as usual, repelled. Again Gregor embraces banishment: "if only the door were opened he would disappear at once." He continues to blame himself for his plight, his sense of inadequacy ("shame and guilt") sharpened by his present failure to attend to his job. His father, at the same time, has grown in dignity to the same degree that Gregor has lost it; in the first month that passes after the metamorphosis, the elder Samsa experiences a change of his own, developing from a feeble, aging dependent to a militant family leader complete with a "smart blue uniform with gold buttons." By the conclusion of the second part he joins with his wife "in complete union" to force Gregor, whom he has wounded, back to his room.

THE FINAL LOCKED DOOR

The last section of the story, while maintaining a narrative form analogous to the preceding parts, offers a version of Gregor's "situation" that is generally more hopeless. At first the father feels some mild compunction: the injury he inflicted reminds him "that Gregor was a member of the family, despite his present unfortunate and repulsive shape, and ought not to be treated as an enemy, that, on the contrary, family duty required the suppression of disgust and the exercise of patience,

---

THE SICKBED

Gregor's bed, a sickbed in The Metamorphosis, *is symbolic of Kafka's own sickbed, in which he died of tuberculosis.*

In *The Metamorphosis,* Gregor Samsa is in bed when he awakens transformed into a vermin. As bizarre as this misadventure is, Kafka tells it as naturally as he would have declared that Gregor had been stricken with smallpox or leprosy. Kafka saw no necessity for giving the last explanation—even an imaginary one—and the rest of the story unfolds in a logical, tragically simple manner. . . .

Is Gregor Samsa's bed simply a sickbed?

The extraordinary importance of sickness in Kafka's work is in a sense a test of its artistic stature. If the novel is an esthetic game for its author and an entertainment for its public, it goes without saying that sickbeds and the sufferings of their occupants amount merely to a romanesque theme. An exception to this rule can scarcely be found, except in a few powerfully realistic works, for sickness is the bitterest and the most sordid of concrete images of reality.

Thus we find another remarkable indication of Kafka's realism in that long row of beds that appears through his work. In them can be seen a new, intimate link between Kafka's writings and his life: these imaginary beds represent the presentiment if not the direct projection of Kafka's own bed in which he died gnawed by tuberculosis after having dragged on with the disease for years.

Excerpted from "Physical Destruction," by Michel Carrouges, in *Kafka Versus Kafka* by Michel Carrouges. Alabama: University of Alabama Press, 1968.

nothing but patience." In "compensation" therefore, he allows the door between Gregor's bedroom and the living room to stand ajar for an hour or two each evening so his son may observe—from within the bedroom—the family's activities. After each such occasion, unfortunately, "his mother, pointing towards his room, said: 'Shut that door now, Grete,' and he was left again in darkness." Gregor "was often haunted by the idea that next time the door opened he would take the family's affairs in hand again"; but in time he finds *their* doings as noxious as they find his ("not one of them thought of shutting the door to spare him such a spectacle and so much noise"). Now when Grete enters his room he "stayed motionless where he was, as if the door had never been opened." Even the three outlandish lodgers, the last set of strangers to enter the house, leave him unaffected—"reconciled . . . to the shutting of the door." This loss of concern for others accompanies his loss of concern for himself; Gregor gradually sinks into an immobilizing "indifference to everything" except his sister's violin playing, which briefly creates an illusion that "the way [was] opening before him to the unknown nourishment he craved." Both parties accept the fact of irreversible estrangement: "'If he could understand us,' said her father, half questioningly; Grete, still sobbing, vehemently waved a hand to show how unthinkable that was." After a final foray from the bedroom, Gregor ends his shame by dying alone behind his doors. And when he disappears for the last time, Grete "turned the key in the lock."

The conclusion of "The Metamorphosis" is ironic: once Gregor is dead, his window, the doors opening into his room, and the outside doors of the apartment are all thrown open with an air of celebration. The lodgers, who like Gregor had disrupted the home, are (like Gregor) ejected; the father completes his conversion to a state of youthful vigor and authority; and Grete changes from a rather indistinct personality to a blooming, outward-looking young lady. "With a frightful slamming of doors," the charlady also departs from the Samsa residence, having disposed of the quickly-forgotten, dried-out corpse. The family finds it possible to unite and to discover new sources of happiness only after the suffering and death of its mainstay. If we take Gregor's incarnation as a roach to indicate figuratively his habitual mental attitude—if we assume, that is, that Kafka meant the physical condition after the transformation to reflect the internal condition before the change—then a spiritual metamorphosis can be said to occur to every Samsa *except* Gregor.

Needless to say, further ethical and psychological implications may be drawn from this triple-tiered fable. What seems clear is that Gregor has projected his life energies wholly into a familial arena: for him there is almost literally no outside existence beyond the cramped room of the private self and the surrounding realms of his family. He sees his moral duty in terms of working to maintain the household; displacing an aged father from that obligation measures the extent of his manliness, while protecting a gentle sister and mother measures the extent of his tenderness. Each side in this introverted relationship feels suffocated and inhibited by the mutual dependence, but neither can imagine a constructive remedy or even understand the position of the other. Both the elder Samsa and Grete come to express resentment, horror, and intolerance at an incomprehensible threat to what should have been a comfortable family hierarchy. "If this were Gregor," the father argues, "he would have realized long ago that human beings can't live with such a creature, and he'd have gone away on his own accord." His resurgence after wounding his son attests to the validity of this judgment. Gregor, of course, understands with greater acuteness both the pernicious consequence of his presence and the lack of alternative.

> He felt great pride in the fact that he had been able to provide such a life for his parents and sister in such a fine flat. But what if all the quiet, the comfort, the contentment were now to end in horror?

> The decision that he must disappear was one that he held to even more strongly than his sister, if that were possible.

The roach (or "dung-beetle") metaphor appropriately symbolizes Gregor's attitude, which in its excessive restrictiveness can be considered to be parasitical. This image reflects Gregor's insecurity and self-loathing: while he needs the emotional sustenance his family can supply, he feels himself—and perhaps the need also—too base and repugnant to deserve anything but negligible gratification. The door image is equally appropriate to the unsuccessful but thrice-repeated effort to extend past the confining wall of self toward sustaining interchange with those Gregor loves. He is unable to communicate, much less to satisfy his desire for "help" either in private areas (bedrooms) or in a common ground (the living room). Only from within his own room, sometimes through an open door, more often through a closed door, can he relate to the family—that is, from a distance and blocked by a barrier interfering with real "union." His confinement necessarily ends in desiccation and death, both in physical and psychological terms; indeed, one signifies the other. The door in "The Metamorphosis," configuring the story's terrifying subject, does not allow easy access between adjacent individuals. Instead, it cuts off intimacy, makes the sound of human voices indistinct, and finally locks a lonely being in upon himself.

Allusions to Christ in *The Metamorphosis*

Suzanne Wolkenfeld

Suzanne Wolkenfeld is Assistant Professor of English at Fordham University. Wolkenfeld discusses the allusions to Christ that appear in *The Metamorphosis*. Gregor is both a seeker and giver of salvation. He makes the self-sacrificing commitment to help send his sister to college to study music, he longs for spiritual sustenance, and he dies by a kind of crucifixion under the weight of his family's persecution and neglect. Unlike Christ, however, Gregor does not rise upward toward divine salvation but sinks further downward to the level of an animal.

The profound resonance of Kafka's "The Metamorphosis" derives from the multiplicity of the meanings of Gregor Samsa's transformation into an insect. This symbolic multivalency resembles that of the dream image in which a variety of often incongruous meanings are condensed. The bizarre event that the story depicts is, in fact, presented as a dream come true, a realization of the uncouscious feelings that trouble Gregor Samsa's sleep. Gregor's metamorphosis emerges as an externalization of his abject insect-like existence as a commercial traveler; as a regression into a primitive state motivated by his desire to escape the burden of tedious responsibility and the painfulness of the human condition; as a manifest sign of his alienation from himself and others. These patterns of meaning have been generally acknowledged and amply documented. The purpose of this note is to explore yet another meaning suggested by allusions to the Christ story. This Christian symbolism, which has probably gone unnoticed because it is sparsely sketched, is an essential element of the ironic pathos that pervades the final section of the work. Moreover, it provides another il-

From "*The Metamorphosis*," by Suzanne Wolkenfeld, Notes section of *Studies in Short Fiction*, vol. 10, no. 2 (Spring 1973), pp. 205–207. Reprinted with permission from *Studies in Short Fiction*.

lustration of Kafka's tendency to project psychological drama into a theological perspective.

In the first two chapters of "The Metamorphosis," Kafka sets up certain parallels between Gregor and Christ that are later developed as an ironic parody. Gregor finds relief from his sterile servitude as a commercial traveler in doing fretwork. As a carpenter of sorts, he shadows Christ. A more substantial resemblance is established by Gregor's plan to culminate his self-sacrificing commitment to his family with a gift for his sister. On Christmas Day he will announce his decision to send her to the Conservatorium to study music. Gregor's Christmas annunciation takes on the coloring of a redemptive act as Kafka proceeds to associate music with salvation.

Gregor is presented not only as a potential savior but also as a seeker of salvation. His longing for a more sustaining mode of life is reflected in his gradual loss of interest in any of the food offered him. Gregor points to the difference between his spiritual yearnings and the desires of people satisfied with the stuff of this life when he witnesses the lodgers enjoying their dinner: "'I'm hungry enough,' said Gregor sadly to himself, 'but not for that kind of food. How these lodgers are stuffing themselves, and here I am dying of starvation!'"

Gregor's spiritual quest culminates in a scene in which music and food fuse into an image of salvation. Lured from his room by the sound of his sister's violin, he is mystically transported by the music and glimpses the salvation he has been seeking: "Was he an animal, that music had such an effect upon him? He felt as if the way were opening before him to the unknown nourishment he craved." Gregor's search for salvation is a failure. Cruelly rebuffed by the family, he returns to his room and resolves to die and thus rid them of their burden.

GREGOR'S CRUCIFIXION

The description of Gregor's death, though rooted in the family drama, is pervaded by crucifixion imagery:

> The rotting apple in his back and the inflamed area around it, all covered with soft dust, already hardly troubled him. He thought of his family with tenderness and love. The decision that he must disappear was one that he held to even more strongly than his sister, if that were possible. In this state of vacant and peaceful meditation he remained until the tower clock struck three in the morning. The first broadening of light in the world outside the window entered his consciousness once more. Then his head sank to the floor of its own accord and from his nostrils came the last faint flicker of his breath.

The pain of the "rotten apple" and "soft dust," representative of his family's persecution and neglect, recede before a new spirit of forgiveness and love. As the apple and dust are emblematic of man's fallen state, Gregor's magnanimity is suggestive of Christ's ushering in the new dispensation. Gregor dies at the end of March at three o'clock, the time of the crucifixion, and his last gesture echoes the gospel description of Christ's death: "He bowed down his head and died."

The pathos of Gregor's "crucifixion" is both intensified and undercut by ironic inflections. The subtle reminders of Gregor's primitive insect nature as he dies undermines his resemblance to Christ. Gregor's state of "vacant and peaceful meditation" suggests not spiritual exaltation but the mindless vacuity of an animal. His dying gesture reminds us of the mechanical instinct that has replaced human will. He does not "bow" his head like Christ; it sinks to the floor "of its own accord."

Other discrepancies serve to further deflate the spiritual implications of the Christ parallel. Gregor dies not at three P.M., the hour of Christ's death, but at three A.M. No miraculous eclipse of the sun accompanies his death, but rather the natural rising of the sun. Instead of a spirit departing from his body, a flicker of breath leaves his nostrils. The death throes of a gigantic insect constitute a grotesque burlesque of Christ's crucifixion.

Kafka develops the consequences of Gregor's sacrifice in the same ironic mode. The family casts off its feelings of guilt as Mr. Samsa persuades the others to "let bygones be bygones." And with a spirit of revitalization, they set out to the country. But we have no sense of uplift at the new life Gregor's death has brought them. The family remains to us commonplace and unsympathetic.

Christ, like Gregor, undergoes a metamorphosis. As a mingling of the divine and the human, he represents the possibility of transcendence for man. Gregor's metamorphosis refutes this possibility. In his quest for salvation, Gregor does not rise upward toward the divine but sinks downward to an animal level. He is a martyr but his suffering is not redemptive. Through the ironic parallel of Gregor to Christ, Kafka points to the tragic discrepancy between the spiritual aspirations and animal limitations of man's nature.

CHAPTER 2

Themes in *The Metamorphosis*

READINGS ON
THE METAMORPHOSIS

The Death of an Outcast

Martin Greenberg

Martin Greenberg is Professor of English at Long Island University. He specializes in writing about science fiction and is the author of *Coming Attractions* and several science fiction anthologies. In the following essay, Greenberg describes Gregor Samsa as an outcast who craves spiritual nourishment. Gregor is cut off from any nurturing human associations within his family or in society; he holds a meaningless and degrading job, and his metamorphosis represents his self-condemnation of his defeated humanity. Unable to find the spiritual nourishment he seeks, Gregor gives up hope of rejoining the human community and strives for a chance of salvation through his banishment, his life as an outcast. Ultimately, however, spiritual starvation takes its toll, and Gregor, Kafka's quintessential antihero, dies unredeemed.

Kafka's *Metamorphosis* is peculiar as a narrative in having its climax in the very first sentence: "As Gregor Samsa awoke one morning from uneasy dreams he found himself transformed in his bed into a gigantic insect." The rest of the *novella* falls away from this high point of astonishment in one long expiring sigh, punctuated by three sub-climaxes (the three eruptions of the bug from the bedroom). How is it possible, one may ask, for a story to start at the climax and then merely subside? What kind of story is that? The answer to this question is, I think—a story for which the traditional Aristotelian form of narrative (complication and dénouement) has lost any intrinsic necessity and which has therefore evolved its own peculiar form out of the very matter it seeks to tell. *The Metamorphosis* produces its own form out of itself. The traditional kind of narrative based on the drama of dénouement—on the "unknot-

From *The Terror of Art: Kafka and Modern Literature*, by Martin Greenberg (New York: BasicBooks, 1968). Reprinted by permission of the author.

ting" of complications and the coming to a conclusion—could not serve Kafka because it is just exactly the absence of dénouement and conclusions that is his subject matter. His story is about death, but death that is without dénouement, death that is merely a spiritually inconclusive petering out.

The first sentence of *The Metamorphosis* announces Gregor Samsa's death and the rest of the story is his slow dying. In its movement as an inexorable march toward death it resembles Tolstoy's *Death of Ivan Ilyich.* As Ivan Ilyich struggles against the knowledge of his own death, so does Gregor Samsa. But Tolstoy's work is about death literally and existentially; Kafka's is about death in life. Until Ivan Ilyich stops defending his life to himself as a good one and recognizes that it hasn't been what it ought to have been, he can't accept the knowledge that he is dying; finally he embraces the truth of his life, which is at the same time the truth of death, and discovers spiritual light and life as he dies. Kafka's protagonist also struggles against "the truths of life and death"; in Gregor Samsa's case, however, his life *is* his death and there is no salvation. For a moment, it is true, near the end of his long dying, while listening to his sister play the violin, he feels "as if the way were opening before him to the unknown nourishment he craved"; but the nourishment remains unknown, he is locked into his room for the last time and he expires.

What Gregor awakens to on the morning of his metamorphosis is the truth of his life. His ordinary consciousness has lied to him about himself; the explosive first sentence pitches him out of the lie of his habitual self-understanding into the nightmare of truth. "*The Metamorphosis* is a terrible dream, a terrible conception," Kafka's young friend Janouch had said to him in one of their conversations. "Kafka stood still. 'The dream reveals the reality, which conception lags behind. That is the horror of life—the terror of art.'"

A DEFEAT OF HUMANITY

What, then, is the truth of Gregor's life? There is first of all his soul-destroying job, which keeps him on the move and cuts him off from the possibility of real human associations. . . .

Not only is his work lonely and exhausting, it is also degrading. Gregor fails to report to work once in five years and the chief clerk is at his home at a quarter past seven in the morning accusing him of neglect of his business duties, poor work in general and stealing company funds, and threatening him with dismissal. In the guilt-world that Gregor inhabits, his missing his train on this one morning retroactively changes his excellent work record at one stroke into the very opposite. . . .

He has been sacrificing himself by working at his meaningless, degrading job so as to pay off an old debt of his parents' to his employer. Otherwise "I'd have given notice long ago, I'd have gone to the chief and told him exactly what I think of him." But even now, with the truth of his self-betrayal pinning him on his back to his bed, he is unable to claim himself for himself and decide to quit—he must wait "another five or six years.". . .

He pretends that he will get up and resume his old life. He will get dressed "and above all eat his breakfast," after which the "morning's delusions" will infallibly be dissipated. But the human self whose claims he always postponed and continues to postpone, is past being put off, having declared itself negatively by changing him from a human being into an insect. His metamorphosis is a judgment on himself by his defeated humanity.

Gregor's humanity has been defeated in his private life as much as in his working life. His mother succinctly describes its deathly aridity as she pleads with the chief clerk:

> . . . he's not well, sir, believe me. What else would make him miss a train! The boy thinks about nothing but his work. It makes me almost cross the way he never goes out in the evenings; he's been here the last eight days and has stayed at home every single evening. He just sits there quietly at the table reading a newspaper or looking through railway timetables. The only amusement he gets is doing fretwork. For instance, he spent two or three evenings cutting out a little picture frame; you would be surprised to see how pretty it is; it's hanging in his room; you'll see it in a minute when Gregor opens the door.

The picture in the little frame shows a woman in furs "holding out to the spectator a huge fur muff into which the whole of her forearm had vanished"; it is the second object that Gregor's eye encounters when he surveys his room on waking (the first was his collection of samples). Later in the story, when his sister and mother empty his room of its furniture, he defends his "human past" by making his stand on this picture, pressing "himself to the glass, which was a good surface to hold on to and comforted his hot belly." That is about what Gregor's "human past" amounts to: a pin-up.

A Stranger in the Family

For most of the story, Gregor struggles with comic-terrible pathos against the metaphor fastened on him. His first hope is that it is all "nonsense." But he can't tell; the last thing he knows about is himself. So he works himself into an upright position in order to unlock the door, show himself to the chief clerk and his family and let them decide for him, as he has always let others decide for him. . . .

The answer that he gets is his mother's swoon, the chief clerk's hurried departure, in silent-movie style, with a loud "Ugh!" and his father's driving him back "pitilessly," with a newspaper and a walking stick that menaces his life, into his room—"from behind his father gave him a strong push which was literally a deliverance and he flew far into the room, bleeding freely. The door was slammed behind him with the stick, and then at last there was silence."

This is the first repulse the metamorphosed Gregor suffers in his efforts to re-enter "the human circle." The fact that his voice has altered so that the others can no longer understand what he says, but he can understand them as well as ever, perfectly expresses the pathos of one who is condemned to stand on the outside looking in. Although he must now accept the fact that he has been changed into a monster, he clings to the illusion that his new state is a temporary one: "he must lie low for the present and, by exercising patience and the utmost consideration, help the family to bear the inconvenience he was bound to cause them in his present condition." Like Ivan Ilyich, he wants to believe that his mortal illness is only a "condition."

In Part II we learn about Gregor's all-important relations with his family. An unambiguous indication already given in Part I is the fact that he locks his bedroom doors at night "even at home"—a "prudent habit he had acquired in traveling." Although he is a dutiful, self-sacrificing son, . . . he is as much a stranger to his family as he is to the world and shuts them out of his life—he locks them out as much as they lock him in. Concealment, mistrust and denial mark the relations in the Samsa family. It now turns out, as Gregor listens at his bedroom door, that some investments had survived the wreck of Samsa Sr.'s business five years before and had even increased since then, though he thought his father had been left with nothing, "at least his father had never said anything to the contrary, and of course he had not asked him directly." Moreover, this sum had been increased by the unexpended residue of Gregor's earnings, who "kept only a few dollars for himself." But he buries the rage he feels at this evidence of the needlessness of his self-sacrifice, as he has always buried his real feelings. . . .

His parents liked to think that his slaving at his job to support the family represented no sacrifice of himself—"they had convinced themselves in the course of years that Gregor was settled for life in this firm." But they were able to convince themselves of this only because he himself cooperated eagerly with them to deny himself. Deception and self-deception, denial and self-denial now "end in horror." To cap it all, it turns out that his family didn't even need his sacrifice for another reason; when Gregor ceases to be the breadwinner, father, mother and sister all turn to and provide for themselves and the old man is even rescued in this way from a premature dotage.

The decisive figure in the family for Gregor is his father, . . . a combination of weakness and strength, signalled in the story's very first words about Samsa Sr.: "at one of the side doors his father was knocking, gently (*schwach*: weakly), yet with his fist." The combination is present in the description of the father's response to Gregor's first breaking out of his bedroom; a "knotted fist" and "fierce expression" go along with tears of helplessness and humiliation. . . .

But in spite of his "great chest," in spite of his voice's sounding "no longer like the voice of one single father" when he drives his son back into his room, in spite of Gregor's being "dumbfounded at the enormous size of his shoe soles" the second time his father chases him back into his room, the elder Samsa . . . does not loom large like a Titanic figure. He is powerful, irascible and petulant, but not mythically powerful. His shoe soles seem "enormous" to his son because of his insect angle of vision—not because the old man is superhuman but because the son is less than human. Everything in the story is seen from Gregor's point of view, the point of view of somebody who has fallen below the human level.

The father's strength is the ordinary strength of human life, which has been temporarily dimmed by his business failure and his son's unnatural ascendancy as the breadwinner of the family. . . . There is no battle; Gregor cannot "risk standing up to him." The unnatural state of affairs in the Samsa home corrects itself so to speak naturally, by the son's showing forth as what he really is—a parasite that saps the father's and the family's life. A fundamental incompatibility exists between the son and the family, between sickliness and parasitism on the one hand and vigor and independence on the other, between death and life. As the son's life wanes the family's revives; especially the father's flourishes with renewed vigor and he becomes a blustering, energetic, rather ridiculous man—a regular Kafka papa.

From the start Gregor's father deals brutally with him:

> . . . from the very first day of his new life . . . his father believed only the severest measures suitable for dealing with him.

Indeed he threatens his life: the first time he shoos Gregor back into his room he menaces him with a "fatal blow" from his stick; at his son's second outbreak he gives him a wound from which he never recovers. But though Samsa Sr. throws his son back into his room two out of the three times he breaks out of it, Gregor's banishment from "the human circle" is not a sentence passed on him by his father. . . . Samsa Sr. does not stand at the center of the story confronting his son as the lord and judge of his life. He stands with the mother and the sister, opposite the son but to the side; the center of the story is completely occupied by the son. The father affirms the judgment passed on Gregor—that he is "unfit for life"—but the judgment is not his; it is Gregor's. At the beginning of the *novella*, before he is locked in his room by the family as a metamorphosed monster, we see how he has already locked himself in as a defeated human being. Gregor is *self*-condemned.

DISGUST AND SELF-DISGUST

At the side of the father stands the mother, gentle ("That gentle voice!"), yet "in complete union with him" against her son. Gregor's monstrousness horrifies her no less than the others and she faints at the sight of him. For the first two weeks she prefers, with the father, not to know how or even if Gregor is fed. "Not that they would have wanted him to starve, of course, but perhaps they could not have borne to know more about his feeding than from hearsay. . . ."—Gregor's struggle, in these words, against the truth is a pathetically ironical statement of it. Mrs. Samsa pities her son—"he is my unfortunate son"—and understands his plight as illness; the morning of the metamorphosis she sends the daughter for the doctor, while Mr. Samsa, characteristically (his son is a recalcitrant creature bent on causing him a maximum of annoyance), sends the maid for the locksmith. (Gregor, feeling "himself drawn once more into the human circle" by these steps, "hoped for great and remarkable results from both the doctor and the locksmith, without really distinguishing precisely between them"—agreeing with both parents, he is unable to distinguish between the element of recalcitrance and refusal and the element of illness in his withdrawal into inhuman isolation.) Shame and horror, however, overwhelm the mother's compassion—we learn from Gregor's reflections that the doctor was sent away on some pretext. She protests against Grete's clearing the furniture out of Gregor's room—". . . doesn't it look as if we were showing him, by taking away his furniture, that we have given up hope of his ever getting better . . . ?"—but then acquiesces weakly in it and even helps to move the heavy pieces. At the end, when Grete says that the bug must be got rid of—

> "He must go," cried Gregor's sister, "that's the only solution, Father. You must just try to get rid of the idea that this is Gregor. . . . If this were Gregor, he would have realized long ago that human beings can't live with such a creature, and he'd have gone away on his own accord."

the mother, with a terrible silence, acquiesces again in her daughter's determination, which this time is a condemnation of her son to death.

Gregor cherishes his sister most of all. She in turn shows the most awareness of his needs after his metamorphosis into vermin and he is grateful to her for it. But he notices that she avoids touching anything that has come into contact with him and he is forced to "realize how repulsive the sight of him still was to her, and that it was bound to go on being repulsive." For her, too, he is a pariah, a monster shut out of the human circle, and at the end she is the one who voices the thought, which has hung unexpressed over the family since the morning of the metamorphosis, that Gregor must be got rid of.

This, then, is the situation in the Samsa family revealed by the metamorphosis: on the surface, the official sentiments of the parents and the sister toward Gregor, and of Gregor toward them and toward himself; underneath, the horror and disgust, and self-disgust: ". . . family duty required the suppression of disgust and the exercise of patience, nothing but patience."

Gregor breaks out of his room the first time hoping that his transformation will turn out to be "nonsense"; the second time, in the course of defending at least his hope of returning to his "human past." His third eruption, in Part III, has quite a different aim. The final section of the story discovers a Gregor who tries to dream again, after a long interval, of resuming his old place at the head of the family, but the figures from the past that now appear to him—his boss, the chief clerk, travelling salesmen, a chambermaid ("a sweet and fleeting memory"), etc., etc.—cannot help him, "they were one and all unapproachable and he was glad when they vanished." Defeated, he finally gives up all hope of returning to the human community. Now his existence slopes steeply toward death. The wound in his back, made by the apple his father threw at him in driving Gregor back into his room after his second outbreak, has begun to fester again; his room is now the place in which all the household's dirty old decayed things are thrown, along with Gregor, a dirty old decayed thing; and he has just about stopped eating.

At first he had thought he was unable to eat out of "chagrin over the state of his room"—his mood at that stage of his dying, like Ivan Ilyich's at a corresponding stage, was one of hatred toward his family for neglecting him; he hissed at them all in rage. But then he discovered that he got "increasing enjoyment" from crawling about the filth and junk—it wasn't the filthiness of his room that was preventing him from eating. On the last evening of his life, watching from his room the lodgers whom his family have taken in putting away a good supper, he comes to a crucial realization:

> "I'm hungry enough," said Gregor sadly to himself, "but not for that kind of food. How these lodgers are stuffing themselves, and here am I dying of starvation!"

In giving up at last all hope of re-entering the human circle, Gregor finally understands the truth about his life—which is to say he accepts the knowledge of his death, for the truth about his life is his death-in-life by his banishment and self-banishment from the human community. But having finally accepted the truth, having finally bowed to the yoke of the metaphor that he has been trying to shake off, he begins to sense a possibility that exists for him *only* in his outcast state. He is hungry enough, he realizes, but not for the world's fare, "not for that kind of food." He feels a hunger that can only be felt in full acceptance of his outcast state. Like Ivan Ilyich when he accepts his death at last and plunges into the black sack's hole, he perceives a glimmer of light; in the degradation, in the utter negativity of his outcastness, he begins to apprehend a positive possibility.

A POSITIVE POSSIBILITY

He has already had a hint or two that the meaning of his metamorphosis contains some sort of positive possibility. At the beginning of the story, when he is lying in bed and worrying
about not reporting to work, he thinks of saying he is sick, but
knows that the sick-insurance doctor will come down on him
as a malingerer. "And would he be so far from wrong on this
occasion? Gregor really felt quite well . . . and he was even unusually hungry." He has just been changed into a huge bug
and he is afraid of pleading sick because he will be accused of
malingering! And the accusation would after all be correct because he felt quite well and was even unusually hungry! "Of
course," the reader says, "he means quite well *as an insect*!"—
which is a joke, but a joke that points right to the positive
meaning of his metamorphosis.

A second hint soon follows. After Gregor unlocks the bedroom door with his jaws and drops down on his legs for the
first time, he experiences "a sense of physical comfort; his legs
had firm ground under them; . . . they even strove to carry him
forward in whatever direction he chose; and he was inclined
to believe that a final relief from all his sufferings was at
hand." The first meaning here is ironical and comic: Gregor,
unable to accept his transformation into a bug and automati-
cally trying to walk like a man, inadvertently falls down on his
insect legs and feels an instantaneous sense of comfort which
he takes as a promise of future relief from his sufferings—with
supreme illogic he derives a hope of release from his animal
condition from the very comfort he gets by adapting himself to
that condition: so divided is his self-consciousness from his
true self. But there is a second meaning, which piles irony
upon the irony: *precisely* as a noisome outcast from the human
world Gregor feels the possibility of relief, of *final* relief. *Only*
as an outcast does he sense the possibility of an ultimate salvation rather than just a restoration of the *status quo*.

As a bug, too, his wounds heal a lot faster than did his old
cut finger: the vitality possible to him in his pariah state (if he
can only find the food he needs to feed his spiritual hunger on:
for he is "unusually hungry") is in sharp contrast with his human debility. And he finds a kind of freedom in crawling
around the walls and ceiling of his room instead of going to
work each morning—Kafka dwells so much in the first part on
the horror of Samsa's job that we feel his metamorphosis as

something of a liberation, although in the end he is only delivered from the humiliation and death of his job into the humiliation and death of his outcast state.

When Gregor breaks out of his room the third and last time, he is no longer trying to deceive himself about himself and get back to his old life with its illusions about belonging to the human community. He is trying to find that "final relief" which lies beyond "the last earthly frontier" (to quote a phrase from Kafka's diary), a frontier which is to be approached only through exile and solitude. What draws him out of his room the last night of his life is his sister's violin playing. Although he had never cared for music in his human state, now the notes of the violin attract him surprisingly. Indifferent to "his growing lack of consideration for the others"— at last he has the courage to think about himself—trailing "fluff and hair and remnants of food" which he no longer bothers to scrape off himself, the filthy starving underground creature advances onto "the spotless floor of the living room" where his sister is playing for the three lodgers.

> Was he an animal, that music had such an effect upon him? He felt as if the way were opening before him to the unknown nourishment he craved.

It is a familiar Romantic idea that Kafka is making use of here: that music expresses the inexpressible, that it points to a hidden sphere of spiritual power and meaning. It is only in his extremity, as "an animal," an outcast from human life who finally accepts his being cast out, that Gregor's ears are opened to music. Yet in spite of all the hints he has had, Gregor still hesitates to grasp the positive possibility contained in the truth about himself and his death in life—the possibility of life in death, of spiritual life *through* outcastness. All along he has understood the wellbeing he feels as an insect as an indication of his bestialization. "Am I less sensitive now?" he asks himself after marvelling at his recuperative powers as a bug; he accuses himself of a growing lack of consideration for others, etc., etc. Now he does the same thing: "Was he an animal, that music had such an effect upon him?" This time, however, his understanding of himself is clearly a misunderstanding; it is nonsensical to associate music and bestiality, music is at the opposite pole from bestiality. His metamorphosis is a path to the spiritual rather than the bestial. The violin notes that move him so build a way through his death in life to the salvation for which he blindly hungers.

Or they only seem to. Certainly the unknown nourishment exists; the goal of his hunger exists. But the music merely draws him toward his sister with the jealous intention of capturing her for himself and immuring her in his cell with him; it only leads him out into the same old living room of his death as a private person, which with the three indignant lodgers staring down at him is the same old public world of bullying businessmen he knew as a travelling salesman. "There is a goal, but no way," Kafka says in one of his aphorisms; "what we call a way is only wavering."

His final repulse follows, with his sister demanding that "he must go. . . . If this were Gregor, he would have realized long ago that human beings can't live with such a creature. . . . " Painfully turning around, Gregor crawls back into his room without his father's having to chase him back and surrenders his life to this demand:

> "And what now?" said Gregor to himself, looking round in the darkness. . . . He thought of his family with tenderness and love. The decision that he must disappear was one that he held to even more strongly than his sister, if that were possible. In this state of vacant and peaceful meditation he remained until the tower clock struck three in the morning. The first broadening of light in the world outside the window entered his consciousness once more. Then his head sank to the floor of its own accord and from his nostrils came the last faint flicker of his breath.

A SPIRITUAL STARVATION

Gregor Samsa dies reconciled with his family in a tenderness of self-condemnation. . . . Nobody sentences Gregor to his death in life except himself. His ultimate death, however, his death without redemption, is from hunger for the unknown nourishment he needs. What kills Gregor is spiritual starvation—"Man cannot live without a permanent trust in something indestructible in himself, and at the same time that indestructible something as well as his trust in it may remain permanently concealed from him," Kafka writes in an aphorism.

Although the story does not end with Gregor's death, it is still from his point of view that the last few pages, with their terrible irony and pathos, are narrated. The family are of course glad to be freed of the burden and scandal he has been to them but dare not say so openly. When the tough old charwoman who has survived "the worst a long life could offer" spares them the embarrassment of getting "rid of the thing," their thanks is to fire her. However the tide of life, now flooding in, soon sweeps them beyond bad conscience and troubled reflections. They make a holiday of Gregor's death day and take a trolley ride into the country. Spring is in the air; a review of their prospects shows them to be "not at all bad." Mother and father notice how their daughter, in spite of everything, has

> bloomed into a pretty girl with a good figure. They grew quieter and half unconsciously exchanged glances of complete agreement, having come to the conclusion that it would soon be time to find a good husband for her. And it was like a confirmation of their new dreams and excellent intentions that at the end of their journey their daughter sprang to her feet and stretched her young body.

Life triumphs blatantly, not only over Gregor's unlife but over his posthumous irony—these last lines are entirely without irony. Or if they are ironical it is at Gregor's expense: his moral condemnation of his family here turns into a condemnation of himself.

Self-Alienation in Kafka's *The Metamorphosis*

Walter H. Sokel

Walter H. Sokel is Commonwealth Professor of German and English Literature at the University of Virginia. His many articles on Franz Kafka have appeared in numerous scholarly journals nationwide, and he is the author of *Franz Kafka: Tragik and Ironie* and *Franz Kafka*. To enable readers to better understand Gregor's alienation, Sokel first discusses the role of self-alienation in Marxist theory. Next, he explores the *mythos* of Gregor's strange transformation, the chain of fictional events in the story, presented in their chronological rather than narrative order, beginning with Gregor's father's failed business ventures. Lastly, Sokel explains the role of guilt in Gregor's transformation, the shift in power within the Samsa household, and Gregor's ultimate sacrifice of self-alienation and death, in which he liberates others from himself and, finally, himself from the world.

Kafka's uniqueness as a narrative author lies, among other things, in the literalness with which the metaphors buried in linguistic usage come alive and are enacted in the scenes he presents. . . . By the appellation "vermin," linguistic usage designates the lowest form of human self-contempt. Seeing himself as vermin, and being treated as such by his business and family, the travelling salesman Gregor Samsa literally turns into vermin.

Kafka's narratives enact not only the metaphors hidden in ordinary speech, but also ideas crucial in the history of thought. *The Metamorphosis* is a striking example. Gregor Samsa's transformation into vermin presents self-alienation in a literal way, not merely a customary metaphor become fic-

From "From Marx to Myth: The Structure and Function of Self-Alienation in Kafka's *Metamorphosis*," by Walter H. Sokel, *The Literary Review*, vol. 26, no. 4 (Summer 1983), pp. 485–96. Reprinted by permission of the author.

tional fact. The travelling salesman wakes up one morning and cannot recognize himself. Seeing himself as a gigantic specimen of vermin, he finds himself in a fundamental sense estranged from himself. No manner more drastic could illustrate the alienation of a consciousness from its own being than Gregor Samsa's startled and startling awakening.

The idea of human self-alienation has played a crucial role in modern thought from German classical Idealism to Marxism and Existentialism. . . . This idea always implies the individual's estrangement (*Entfremdung*) from his humanity or "human species being," i.e., from the individual's membership in the human species. The individual is estranged from himself insofar as he is alienated from his essential nature as a human being.

Rooted as he was in German Idealism and the tradition of German classical literature, the young Karl Marx saw the essential nature of the human species residing in freely productive activity. Human species-being was for him the production of objects that were literally *Gegen-stände*, things that having issued from the labor of his hands and mind now face their producer as the objects of his world. Thus the human species is defined by world-creating or world-modifying activity. It is an activity that by virtue of its productive inventiveness humanizes nature. In order to be truly human, this praxis must be, at least partly, self-determined. Work must be engaged in for its own sake. It must have been chosen, partially at least, for its intrinsic pleasure. It must not merely be dictated by external need or the commands of others. In exact analogy to Immanuel Kant's corollary to the categorical imperative, which defines genuine morality, genuinely human labor for Marx must be at least partially its own end, its own freely chosen purpose, and not entirely "a means" for something else such as the satisfaction of extrinsic needs or the insurance of mere survival. To qualify as truly human, labor must always have an element of free choice. It must, at least partly, be its own reward and satisfaction. "At any time" it must "be considered its own purpose, an end in itself."

This freedom of doing one's work for its own sake, for the joy it affords the worker, is the factor that, according to Marx, distinguishes human from animal productivity. Animals, Marx observes, "produce only under the compulsion of physical need. Man, on the other hand, produces even when he is free of physical need, and only in this freedom is he humanly creative. . . . Such production is his active species being. By virtue of it, nature itself appears as man's creation and his reality." Only where work appears as its own reward are human beings truly human. Where it is imposed solely by economic necessity, the worker is not merely alienated from himself as an individual; he is estranged from his humanity. Marx's idea of human self-alienation is not restricted to factory work, but includes any kind of work in which an individual is engaged merely for the wage or income it brings him. The worker is dehumanized wherever his work fails to involve his creative urge and desire.

Here we have arrived at the pre-history of Gregor Samsa's metamorphosis, as the reader learns from Gregor's reminiscences of and meditations about his job as a travelling salesman. We learn that Gregor had been estranged from himself in his all-consuming work even before he finds himself literally estranged from his bodily being. Gregor had found his work unbearable. He had longed for nothing more passionately than to leave his job, after telling the head of his firm his true opinion of this job. Gregor's profound self-alienation corresponds, with uncanny precision, to Marx's definition of the "externalization" of work under capitalism:

> His work is *external* to the worker, i.e., it does not form part of his essential being so that instead of feeling well in his work, he feels unhappy, instead of developing his free physical and mental energy, he abuses his body and ruins his mind.

Gregor Samsa's professional activity has obviously been such purely instrumental work, external to himself, imposed upon him by the necessity of bailing out his bankrupt family, supporting them, and paying back his parents' debt to the boss of his firm. It is not only joyless and uncreative, it is totally determined by needs external to itself and Gregor. Freedom of creativeness—according to Marx the essence of truly human labor—finds an outlet in Samsa's life, prior to his metamorphosis, only in the carpentry in which he indulges in free evenings. Parenthetically we might recall that Kafka himself hated his bureaucrat's desk job because it served as a mere means to a purpose totally extrinsic to itself, namely a relatively short work day, and found by contrast genuine satisfaction in carpentering and gardening, activities chosen for their own sake, which, like writing, united creativeness with the satisfaction of inner needs.

Compared to accusations of his office work found in his autobiographical documents, Kafka's story, *The Metamorphosis*, "systematizes," as it were, the Marxist factor, not by conscious design, of course, but by virtue of the astonishing parallelism in the point of view, particularly the presentation of self-alienation. Gregor's sole reason for enduring the hated position, the need to pay his parents' "debt" to his boss, drastically highlights the doubly extrinsic purpose of Gregor's work. For not only is his labor alien to his true desires, but its sole purpose, its fruit—the salary or commission that it affords him—does not even belong to him. Gregor's toil does not serve his own existence. It is not his own *Lebensmittel*, to use Marx's term—if left to himself, he would have quit long before—it belongs to and serves another.

This other is Gregor's father. He is the non-working beneficiary and exploiter of Gregor's labor. The product of this labor is the money which Gregor brings home. This money belongs to the other who does not work himself, but enjoys and disposes of the fruits of Gregor's work: "the money which Gregor had brought home every month—he himself had kept only a few pennies to himself—had not been used up completely and had accrued to form a small capital." Gregor's father had expropriated the "surplus value" of Gregor's labor and formed with it his—to be sure, very modest—"capital." Gregor's relationship to his father thus represents an exact paradigm of the worker's exploitation by his capitalist employer, as described by Marx. The worker is alienated from the product of his labor because he has to yield it to the capitalist. The latter retains the lion's share for himself and returns to the worker only what the latter barely needs to survive. Through this despoiling of the fruits of his work the worker's existence becomes, in the words of Marx, "self-sacrifice and castigation": "In the last analysis, the extrinsic nature of his work is shown to the worker by the fact that his work is not his, but belongs to another. . . . it is the loss of his self." Gregor's metamorphosis literally enacts this "loss of self." It makes drastically visible the self-estrangement that existed even before his metamorphosis.

It is the father's "capital" that leaves Gregor tied to his servitude and bondage, for as the narrator says, "with this surplus money [Gregor] could have paid back a much larger part of his father's debt to his boss and the day on which he could have freed himself from this job would have been much closer. . . ."

The last-mentioned fact represents a point at which an entirely different interpretative dimension intersects the Marxist framework of self-alienation that we have so far considered by itself. Although we have by no means as yet exhausted the parallelism between the Marxist concept of self-alienation and the structure and function of Gregor Samsa's metamorphosis in Kafka's text, we might state at this point that Kafka's *The Metamorphosis* is by no means completely defined, if merely seen as the literal enactment of self-alienation. . . .

"METAMORPHOSIS" AS MYTH

What we shall consider now is Kafka's *The Metamorphosis* as the telling of a myth, for the mythic dimension relates to the Marxist one the way a picture frame relates to the picture which it contains and transcends, at one and the same time. In order to recognize this relationship, we shall have to consider the *mythos* of *The Metamorphosis*. I use the term "mythos" in the Aristotelian sense as the whole chain of fictive events in their chronological as distinct from their narrated order.

The initial point of the mythos is not Gregor's transformation, but the business failure of Gregor's father five years before. This failure led to the contracting of the burdensome debt to the head of Gregor's firm. Thus the mythos begins with a family's cataclysmic fall into adversity through the fault of the father, more precisely the parents, since the text speaks of "die Schuld der Eltern" and only afterward of "die Schuld des Vaters." The German word *Schuld* signifies debt, guilt, and causative fault. This triple meaning is crucial to the understanding of Kafka's mythos. If understood in the sense of debt, the *Schuld* of Gregor's parents belongs to socio-economic quotidian reality. If understood in the two other senses, *Schuld* belongs to a framework of moral and religious values. The text's repeated use of the singular *Schuld* in contrast to the more customary plural *Schulden* for debt provides a subliminally effective counterpoint to the obvious surface meaning of the word.

This subliminal allusion to guilt receives corroboration from the position of "die Schuld der Eltern" ("the guilt of the parents") at the initial point of the narrative mythos. This position creates a subtle analogy to the fall of mankind as told in Genesis. To be sure, this analogy amounts to the faintest of hints. However, we cannot and must not avoid noting the allusion if we take seriously Kafka's view of language as expressed in one of his aphorisms: "Language can only be used allusively for anything outside the sensory world. . . ."

The son of these guilty parents—Gregor—has to assume their guilt and pay it off "by the sweat of his countenance" (to quote Genesis), by his self-consuming drudgery for his parents' creditor. In the allusive context established by the semantic ambiguity of *Schuld*, Gregor's profoundly alienated existence prior to his metamorphosis establishes the parallel to man's fate after the expulsion from paradise. Like the children of Adam and Eve, Gregor through his sonship in the flesh has been condemned to a perennial debtor's existence. The two semantic realms of *Schuld*—debt and guilt—converge in the fateful consequence of the father's debt. With it, the father surrendered his family to a world in which the exploitation of man by man holds infernal sway. The world to which the father's failing has handed over his family is ruled by the principles of capitalist economics. In this world, the family ceases to be a family in the original and ideal sense of a community in which the bonds of blood—the *Blutkreis* to which Kafka in discussing "The Judgment" accords his highest respect—and natural affection prevail. Instead the family falls victim to the egotistical principle of *gegenseitige Übervorteilung* (mutual defrauding) in which Marx saw the governing principle of human life under capitalism.

Precisely because of his self-sacrifice in assuming his father's debt, Gregor rises to power as the breadwinner in his family and threatens to displace his father as the head of the household. This process reverses itself with Gregor's metamorphosis. Gregor's self-inflicted debasement entails his father's rejuvenation and return to power. These successive displacements—first the father's, then the son's—which find their parallel in Grete's ambiguous liberation through her brother's fall, have their contrastive complements in the parasitic exploitation of the winners by the losers. Before Gregor's metamorphosis, the father was the parasite. After the metamorphosis, the son assumes this role.

A world is shown in which the enjoyment of advantages by the one has to be purchased at the cost of the other. This is the world in a fallen state. Gregor's initial self-sacrifice through work whips up his pride in his ability to support his family in style. Those had been "happy times" when he had been able to "amaze and delight" his family by putting his hard-earned money on their table. But his self-surrender to his work causes a twofold alienation. Inwardly he remains estranged from his work because it is the kind of labor that cannot satisfy a human being. Outwardly his rise to power in the family over-shadows the other members and results in their alienation from him. "A special warmth toward him was no longer forth-coming," so the text informs us. Long before his metamorphosis, Gregor and his family have lived coldly and incommunicatively side by side.

The metamorphosis reveals this alienation in its essence as *den völligen Verlust des Menschen* ("the total dehumanization of man") in which Marx saw the ultimate fate of man under capitalism. But it has another and ultimately more important function. Through it Gregor ceases to treat the *Schuld* of his parents as a debt that can be paid back by work, and assumes the *Schuld* in its deeper meaning. He no longer tries to pay back the *Schuld;* he incorporates it. With his incarnation he raises the narrative mythos from its socio-economic to its mythic meaning.

GREGOR'S GUILT

That Gregor's metamorphosis literally incarnates guilt becomes apparent first of all by the fact that his immediate reaction to his transformation is a guilty conscience. He has missed the hour of his work and feels guilty for it. He feels guilty for having plunged his family into misfortune. He is ashamed. He seeks to hide, to make himself invisible. But even apart from all subjectively felt or morally accountable guilt, guilt becomes evident in him objectively. For his transformation into vermin entails the crassest form of parasitic exploitation, a perfect turning of the tables on his family. His metamorphosis compels them to work for him and in his place. Because of him they will henceforth be "overlooked and overtired," condemned to suffer the fate of "paupers." To be sure, his father's bankruptcy five years before had condemned Gregor to an exploited existence. But by his metamorphosis, Gregor himself turns into an arch exploiter, the archetypal parasite which vermin represents. His very appearance as *ungeheueres Ungeziefer* is emblematic and flaunts a gigantic form of parasitism. Even as Gregor's subsequent daydream of declaring his love to his sister constitutes a gruesome parody of bourgeois-sentimental courtship, so his vermin existence as such embodies exploitation as the essence of human relations. By embodying parasitism in his shape, Gregor objectifies the guilt of his entire society. This guilt had originally shown itself in his father when he secretly cheated his son and furtively put aside his son's earnings to form "a modest capital." Reversing their roles, the son now becomes exploitation in its most honest, clearly visible form. To use T. S. Eliot's term, most appropriate to Kafka's tale, Gregor becomes the "objective correlative" of the insight that exploitation is the original guilt of mankind. Gregor literally becomes what his father had committed in stealthily performed acts.

In the narrative mythos of Kafka's tale, the metamorphosis literally takes the place of the father's debt. The text mentions a debt only for the prehistory of *The Metamorphosis*, as a flashback in Gregor's memory. In the action which the reader witnesses, the debt plays no role. The text never mentions it again. It seems that Gregor's *Schreckgestalt*, his new terrifying shape, which the first morning after his awakening had chased away the deputy of the firm, has thereby also cancelled the parents' debt. In place of it, Gregor himself has become "the misfortune" of the Samsa family.

Later, the father wounds Gregor with an apple which rots and festers in Gregor's flesh. This apple functions not only as a renewed allusion to "the guilt of first parents"; it also signifies the function of Gregor's metamorphosis as the literal incorporation of his father's guilt. Gregor, mortally hurt by the blind "rage" of his father, has obviously become his father's victim in the concluding section of the story. Yet this final violation of the son by the father only repeats in a transparent way Gregor's initial victimization. In the beginning, Gregor had to assume his father's debt and thus become its victim. At that time *Schuld* had been understood in the economic and juridical meaning of debt. By his metamorphosis Gregor incorporates this *Schuld* and transforms it from a legal-contractual concept into its full and profound meaning as the concretely visible form of alienated life. Parenthetically one might say that the *Schuld* which the father bequeathes to the son is in the last analysis life itself. The "rotting apple in the flesh" not only causes, but also embodies Gregor's protracted dying. This seems to suggest that the original "guilt of the parents" was the dubious "gift" of physical existence. This reading would connect *The Metamorphosis* with numerous other works by Kafka and with the spirit of his aphorisms.

In contrast to his father, Gregor does not incur guilt; he is guilt. His incarnation of guilt corresponds to Christ's incarnation of God in man, in one sense only. Like Christ, Gregor takes the cross upon himself to erase "the guilt of the parents." But in contrast to Christ, Gregor does not merely assume suffering by his fellow creatures; he also assumes their guilt. Since he has made guilt identical with himself, he must liberate the world, i.e., his family, from himself.

"The guilt of the parents" showed itself as indebtedness. It constituted capitulation to the world in its capitalist makeup. In strict consequence, economic determination inserts itself now into the myth as Kafka presents it. This insertion can be understood in socio-cultural and, indeed, Marxist categories. The plot inserted into the mythic events depicts a classic case of the proletarianization of a petty-bourgeois household. The "modest capital" created by the father's exploitation of Gregor's work for the firm "sufficed . . . not at all to permit the family to live on its interests." In consequence the family loses its bourgeois status, its economic independence. Father Samsa remains the omnipotent potentate in his family. But in the world outside, he toils as a humble bank messenger. By the self-elimination of her brother as a human being, Grete rises to monopolistic eminence and privilege in her family. But in the outside world, she has to serve strangers as a poor sales girl. Gregor's mother is reduced to taking sewing and dressmaking work home. In regard to the socio-economic world of exploited labor, Gregor, by the horrible paradox that is his metamorphosis, is now the only "free" member of the family, the only one who does not have to labor and let himself be exploited by the world outside.

A SHIFT IN POWER

The family's proletarianization reaches its nadir when it has to yield the control over its household to the three lodgers. According to Marx, as capitalism increasingly absorbs all pre-capitalistic forms of human life, "the contrast between natural and social existence becomes progressively more extreme." In Kafka's tale, the displacement of the "natural," traditional head of the family, the father, by the three strangers exemplifies the development described by Marx. The three lodgers assume the dominant place in the household merely by virtue of their paying power. Kafka's plot mimetically conforms to and expresses Marx's observation of the historic change from blood kinship to money as the determining element in all human relationships. *The Metamorphosis* shows how the basis of power, even within the "natural" unit of the family, slips from blood, age, and sex, the foundations of the father's dominance, to money which makes the unrelated strangers the rulers of the family. The family forfeits its autonomy even within its own walls. Of course, even prior to this loss, the family's independence had been appearance only since the father's debt to Gregor's firm had handed it over to the tyranny of the business world, represented by the creditor's firm. The lodgers' invasion of the household and their assumption of absolute control over it thus, in Marx's words, only "brings to a head" what had been inherent in the family's enslavement to the capitalist world through the father's original guilt. . . .

In *The Metamorphosis*, "the guilt of the parents" has been transferred to Gregor. He is the scapegoat on whom the refuse, the filth, the "sin," of the whole community is deposited. This transference appears in him not only physically and externally as when the *Unrat* of the whole apartment is thrown into his room. It also shows itself inwardly as the—temporary—reprehensible and shocking deterioration of Gregor's character makes clear.

What remains for Gregor to do is to recognize that it is his role and mission "to bear away forever . . . the accumulated misfortunes and sins" of his family by removing himself in whom they are incarnated. In this lies the inner meaning of his metamorphosis which his sister's words make clear to him. "His opinion that he must disappear was if anything even more decided than his sister's."

He literally carries out the "turning," the spatial "return" "back into his room" that transposes *The Metamorphosis* from its economically determined foreground plot into the mythic frame from which it had issued. Hitherto intent on breaking out and returning to power, influence, love, and life, Gregor now withdraws forever into his room, into himself. He gives himself up to death by which he liberates not only the world from himself, but more importantly for Kafka, himself from the world.

The death of Gregor Samsa is self-imposed in the literal sense that it occurs only after the consent of the "hero." Gregor carries out the death sentence on himself that his sister, as the representative of the family and of life, has pronounced against him. He executes it by virtue of what can only be considered psychic power. He kills himself simply by his will—resembling in this respect Kleist's *Penthesilea*. His will is to obey the "law" which has chosen him for sacrifice so that his family can live free of *Schuld*, and the formulation of this will is immediately followed by its fulfillment—Gregor's death. It is a sacrificial death for the family of whom he thinks "with tenderness and love."

The Father-Son Relationship at the Heart of *The Metamorphosis*

Richard H. Lawson

Richard H. Lawson is author of *Edith Wharton* and
Gunther Grass of the Literature and Life: World Writers Series. He has written numerous articles on German literature and Germanic languages and is professor emeritus of German at the University of North
Carolina at Chapel Hill. Lawson explores the unhealthy father-son relationship of Kafka's novella. Gregor, in his transformed state, becomes a virtual prisoner in his own home. Persecuted, repelled, and
physically abused by his father, Gregor is forced to retreat to the solace of his room, where he eventually
dies of starvation, while Mr. Samsa enjoys a life of renewed vigor and vitality.

Kafka wrote *The Metamorphosis* in November and December
1912, thus within two or three months of the night in September when he wrote "The Judgment" in a single sitting. *The
Metamorphosis* took a little longer, three weeks. The composition, moreover, was interrupted by the necessity of superin-
tending the family-owned asbestos factory for two weeks
while the superintendent was on a business trip. To this
rankling interruption, added to his duties in the insurance office, Kafka attributed at least some of his dissatisfaction with
the novella recorded in his diary in late 1913 and early 1914.
Although he had earlier expressed satisfaction with the story,
a year later he found it to be fundamentally—or almost fundamentally—flawed. He branded the ending as "unreadable." It
seems a curious if authentic judgment on a novella that has
become one of the most widely read and discussed works of
twentieth-century literature, a comic tragedy of modern man's
isolation, alienation, inadequacy, and guilt.

Despite Kafka's insistence that the protagonist Gregor Samsa "is not merely Kafka and nothing else," the fictional surname is obviously a cryptogram—Kafka himself notes the similarity—of the author's surname. It is indeed a more precise cryptogram, consonant for consonant, vowel for vowel, than that borne by Raban in "Wedding Preparations in the Country," with whom Gregor shares also the distinction of turning into an insect. In Gregor's case the metamorphosis is different in that it is, first unwilled, second definitive, and third total—that is, there is no split of Gregor's being once he becomes a bug. In short, Gregor Samsa, a traveling salesman who by dint of exhausting labor has been supporting his parents and his sister, awakes one rainy morning after troubled dreams to find himself transformed into a monstrous bug, evidently a beetle or much like a beetle. Unable to go to work, he is virtually held prisoner by his family, while his formerly idle father, with new vigor, resumes work. The loathsome bug is not only held prisoner, kept in his room as much as possible, but he is also violently persecuted by his father. His mother ineffectually pleads for Gregor, and his sister feeds—or tries to feed—her metamorphosed brother. But Gregor fails to find satisfaction or nourishment in the fresh food that she at first places before him. Alternately ignored and persecuted, he gradually starves and dies—to the resurgent joy of his family.

The Metamorphosis, formally structured, has no sense of the incompleteness that marks much of Kafka's fiction—not only the novels. It has three Roman-numbered sections, the latter two each reiterating their predecessors, yet emphasizing and adding as well, and each section ending with its own climax. In the first section when Gregor, already an insect as the story opens, ventures from his bedroom, he is repelled by his enraged father. In the second section, now more reconciled to his insect predicament—preferring, for example, to eat rotten food rather than fresh milk—he is again driven out of the living room by his father and back to his bedroom. From this foray he receives the possibly fatal apple—thrown by his father—lodged in his back. In the third section, attracted as a nonhuman by the spirit emanating from his sister's violin-playing, he is once more driven back to his room where, without his actively willing it, death soon follows—whether brought about by the apple or gradual starvation.

KAFKA'S ALTER EGO

The reader is correct in regarding the father-son relationship—as in "The Judgment"—as basic to *The Metamorphosis*. Indeed it was at one point Kafka's desire to publish these two thematically related novellas, together with "The Stoker," in a single volume under the suggestive title, *Sons*. A more specifically appropriate title would have been "The Estranged Son." But in *The Metamorphosis* Kafka has a much firmer artistic grip both on his estrangement and on his fictional alter ego. That is, he achieves a bit of artistic distance from the unfortunate Gregor Samsa—distance perhaps compelled by the inevitable humor, as well as horror, involved in causing his alter ego to turn into a monstrous bug. In the event, his view of the bug is from the outside and his sympathy is tempered with humor; for example, the bug delights in devouring a piece of cheese that Gregor in human form just two days ago had pronounced inedible.

Conceivably, it is tempting to maintain that Gregor as insect is a delusion on the part of Gregor, that he remains human but imagines himself an insect. Kafka seems to provide little leeway, however, for such an interpretation, declaring forthrightly at the outset of the second paragraph, "It was no dream." Still, it is a valid critical insight that Gregor, as a loathsome insect, has become that which he was made to feel by his family, especially by his father; but also by his employer, by his life as a traveling salesman, by—there is more than ample textual warrant—his society, that is, by exploitive, rapacious, dehumanizing, capitalistic industrial society. His metamorphosis is already an accomplished fact before the story opens. Kafka gives it to the reader whole on the first page and thereafter calmly insists on its reality. Although the reader knows that such a transformation is impossible, he or she probably has been induced by Kafka's skillful dissociation to suspend disbelief.

The kind of bug that Gregor has changed into has excited a bit of speculation. Raban, in "Wedding Preparations in the Country," was (partly) a beetle, in German, *Käfer*. This seems to have led a number of critics to assume that Gregor Samsa was likewise a beetle, an assumption comfortably reinforced by the fact that the cleaning woman employed by the Samsas refers to their metamorphosed son as an "old dung beetle." But to take the coarse and comic cleaning woman's taxonomic view in preference to that of the dispassionate and generally well-informed narrator seems not especially well advised. The narrator, who in Kafka's fiction is pretty obviously Kafka himself, calls the creature *ein ungeheueres Ungeziefer*, of which the noun, *Ungeziefer*, is not very specific at all, something like English "vermin," which some translators prefer to "insect" or "bug." *Ungeheuer(es)* means "monstrous."

It is probably revealing that Kafka uses a noun that inhibits a clear visual image of the bug. Revealing, that is, of the irrelevance of the exact taxonomy of the insect. When Kafka's publisher commissioned an illustration by Ottomar Starke for the story, Kafka inveighed against any depiction of the insect itself: "The insect itself cannot be drawn." His wish evidently was heeded; Starke drew a human figure. . . . The most detailed of Coester's illustrations is of an indeterminate scaly bug measuring perhaps two by three feet, with an array of legs that are highly detailed, irregular, and quasi-human. Among the scales on the lower part of the body is the design of a man's face—the face of the father, as one sees from the other illustrations.

ALIENATION

Of course, the father is the focus of Gregor's alienation—the perpetrator of assaults on him, the thrower of the apple that seems to be at least in part responsible for Gregor's death. It is the father who in the first place is responsible for Gregor's wage-slavery to his pitiless employer, for Gregor's wretched existence as a traveling salesman. For the collapse of his father's business and the resulting debt had obliged Gregor to undertake the support of the family. He did so capably, gradually also working off the debt (his employer was also his father's creditor). But at what a personal cost! No job could have been more demanding, more dehumanizing. And while his father became a layabout, lounging around the flat all day long in his dressing gown, unable to rise in greeting when Gregor returned from a wearying day, Gregor had effectively, unthinkingly supplanted the old man and himself taken over the role of paterfamilias.

Coincident with Gregor's metamorphosis into a bug is the transformation of his prematurely retired father into an active proud breadwinner for his family. Almost forced by circumstance, Gregor had encroached on this paternal preserve—now reclaimed by the pater redivivus (whom the reader compares with the father rampant in "The Judgment"). The father's new position is that of a bank messenger. Even at home he proudly wears the smart blue uniform of his new calling, complete with gold buttons. While Gregor, of course, wears the less-splendid raiment of a repulsive insect—although ironically this may well cover a creature in the process of becoming more human, psychologically speaking, than when he was an automaton-employee.

KAFKA'S LITERATURE REFLECTS HIS ISOLATED LIFE

Kafka lived his life through the characters in his stories and novels, which likewise express the feelings of isolation he suffered as a writer.

Kafka's life is almost empty of incident, apart from his two engagements to Felice Bauer, both of which he broke off. He does not appear to have had formative experiences; he did not make extensive trips or form associations with writers of equal stature. He attended a "good" German-language *Gymnasium* and studied literature briefly at the University of Prague before turning to law. Soon after obtaining his doctoral degree, he took up a position at the state Worker's Accident Insurance Institute, where he stayed until illness forced his retirement. He was a conscientious employee, rising to a position of considerable responsibility. He suffered, however, from the routine and stress of the office, for they interfered with the activity that mattered most—indeed, almost exclusively—to him: his nocturnal writing.

But the matter is more complicated. The *Diaries* go on to record periods of freedom from the office, yet no work accomplished. Kafka cared so much about his writing, felt so intensely its power over him, that he must have wanted to put up resistances to it for fear that it would leave nothing of himself.

Kafka's real history is his life as literature. To understand him, we should substitute the word *literature* for the word *history* in R.G. Collingwood's formula: "History is the life of mind itself which is not mind except so far as it both lives in the historical process and knows itself as so living." The acts of Kafka's real history are his stories and novels, which are at the same time reflections on the act of writing itself. They are, of course, reflections of something else besides—of the cruelty of the family, the coldness of bureaucracy, the misery of cities. But this something else becomes something less if it deprives us of the most intense and coherent experience of Kafka's world. At the center of this world are the feelings of isolation, indebtedness, and shortcoming which mark his existence as a writer—that form of estrangement that tries to maintain itself as estrangement and to take this condition to its limit. Kafka's stories treat questions of personal happiness, social justice, and filial piety from the standpoint of his fate as literature.

Excerpted from (unnamed) editor's epilogue to *The Metamorphosis* by Franz Kafka. New York: Vanguard, 1946.

As a sensitive bug, Gregor has to witness the scene that above all he would rather not see; the father in perfect sexual union with his wife (preceded by a comic tableau vivant of one petticoat after another falling down as the mother, stumbling, hurls herself on the father). The Oedipal component, a given in Kafka's fiction, here finds simultaneously traumatizing, poignant, and comic expression—reflecting the unusual distancing that Kafka has managed to attain in *The Metamorphosis.*

Together with the father's sharp uniform and revived sexual energy goes his insistence on remaining in his seat of power in the living room even when so drunken with sleep that the women of the household must drag and propel him to bed. Sartorially (though the continually worn uniform was picking up grease spots), sexually, physically renascent, he also resumes his management of the family purse—which, thanks to Gregor's former efforts as well as to a reserve fund somehow salvaged from the collapse of the business, is in fact in rather good shape. The reader does not miss the irony in this: the presumably ruinous state of the family finances was after all the reason Gregor had enslaved himself to his employer and become subject to the dehumanization that took literal shape in his transformation into a bug. The elder Samsa fully reasserts his domestic authority by summarily evicting the three boarders who had been usurping the power in the flat, relegating the Samsas to the kitchen to eat their meals. Samsa senior can even afford a little indulgence toward the imprisoned Gregor: he allows the door to Gregor's bedroom to be left ajar so that Gregor might have the solace of watching and listening to his family around the lamp-lit table.

A SPIRITUAL DESIRE

The reestablishment of bourgeois family hegemony under the aegis of the father is signaled by Kafka's nomenclature. Suddenly, well toward the end of part III, on the cleaning woman's shouted report that the insect that was Gregor was quite dead, the father and mother, sitting up in bed, are given back their bourgeois designation: Mr. and Mrs. Samsa. As that unadmirable dual entity they will shortly—after Gregor's body, flat and dry, is swept away—perceive that their daughter Grete is blossoming and shapely. In a word, Grete is highly marriageable, a condition not without its advantage to Mr. and Mrs. Samsa. From an ironic and antibourgeois point of view it could be said that, having sacrificed

Gregor to the system, they are quite prepared to do the same—if in a different way—to Grete.

Grete, one recalls, was the only family member with whom the metamorphosed Gregor had any rapport—and that rapport did not survive the impact of disparity, nor, somewhat more inferentially, her emergence from ebullient girlhood to a more mature awareness of the nature and realities of her world. At first Grete tried conscientiously to do what she could for Gregor: to find out what he would eat, to make him feel comfortable, to anticipate his wishes. She was the family expert on Gregor, his representative, as best she could be, to their uncomprehending mother and their antagonistic and resurgent father. But then she too, burdened by an impossible charge in dealing with the unknown, undergoes, at about sixteen years of age, her own metamorphosis: into a practical-minded young woman who would honor the memory of her brother but who would at the same time want to get rid of the noisome bug that inhabits his room.

The violin-playing episode—and Gregor's reaction to it—is the climax and the symbol of Grete's metamorphosis. The boarders appear to be interested in hearing her play further; an impromptu recital is arranged. Despite her beautiful, soulful playing, however, they become bored and irritated. Not so Gregor, who, profoundly affected, "as if the way were opening before him to the unknown nourishment he craved," crawls forward. No one here appreciates her playing, he reflects, as he would appreciate it if she would come into his room with her violin; he would never let her out, but in any case she would stay of her own free will.

Thus the would-be enlistment of Grete in Gregor's longing for otherworldly nourishment, now more spiritual than alimentary. Gregor certifies the spirituality by reflecting further that only as an insect (an insect unburdened of human materialism) has he been able to be at one with beautiful music—when he was a human being it had meant nothing to him. The reader, however, will also have sensed in Gregor's reflections and fantasies about his sister an incestuous desire. Latent it had doubtless been, while he was in human form; as the music frees his spiritual desire, so also it releases a less spiritual desire.

REJECTION

How long does Grete play to this desire, does she even divine it? One cannot be at all certain. The recital ends when the middle roomer descries Gregor's advance, when the roomers demand explanations; for a while Grete's eyes continue to follow the score after she has stopped playing. Laying the violin in her mother's lap while the roomers announce their intention of leaving "in view of the disgusting conditions," she hastens into their room and in a skillfully managed flurry of pillows and blankets makes their beds and slips out. Thus is symbolized, as the violin slips onto the floor with a reverberating clang, her rejection of Gregor, of her rapport with Gregor, of, possibly, her uncritical adolescence, and on the other hand her acceptance of her domestic, adult function in the real world—her metamorphosis. It is at this point that she dissociates the name of her brother from the insect: "We must try to get rid of it." And later: "It has to go." Gregor is no longer "he," but "it," although some English versions fail to make this important distinction. And as its sister locks it up in Gregor's room, its end is near. Its last glance, on being forced back into its room, is at its mother—now fast asleep after the tumultuous scene.

While Gregor both early and late yearns for his mother, and she after his initial imprisonment began fairly soon to want to visit him, there is no metamorphosis in her case. She remains a somewhat intermediate character: less hostile than the father, not without an occasional flash of insight superior to the sister's, but on the whole unsure of herself, overexcited (but who wouldn't be?), given to asthmatic seizure, anxious to indulge and please her husband—not far from a caricature of the bourgeois housewife that she has been and will be again when the Samsas, prosperous, if fewer in number, find a smaller, more advantageously located apartment. As caricature the mother is outshone only by the bawling cleaning woman with an ostrich feather in her hat, who gleefully reports that she has performed the function of disposing of Gregor's desiccated body. For her, never having known Gregor before his metamorphosis, things are simpler: "it" has always been an "it."

The reader, like the cleaning woman, need perhaps not be unduly grieved at Gregor's death—though for a different reason, namely that of insight. Gregor was unsuited for, dissatisfied with, the normal if extremely burdensome existence that he was obliged to be a part of. Of course, that existence was paradoxical—and hardly happy. But Gregor is incapable of articulating his desire for a different nourishment, and this is as true figuratively as it is literally. He accordingly comes to see that he must disappear. With an apple—fruit of knowledge—

lodged immovably and painfully but perhaps not mortally on his back, he dries up from a not very forcefully willed self-starvation.

Dawn is beginning to lighten the world outside his window as his head sinks to the floor of its own accord and he breathes his last. Penultimate illumination through a window occurs as more than one Kafka hero expires. Some take this as a sign of eschatological hope. Max Brod in particular likes to see such hope in Kafka. Others prefer to see a light through a window, or maybe through a doorway, as a dimension of irony. In Kafka's concept the same light could very well represent at once both hope *and* irony.

Banishment in *The Metamorphosis*

Kimberly Sparks

Kimberly Sparks is the Charles A. Dana Professor of German at Middlebury College, Vermont. She is the author of *German in Review, Modern German,* and *Thomas Mann's 'Tonio Kroger' als Weg zur Literatur.* Sparks explores the theme of banishment in *The Metamorphosis* and illuminates how Kafka's characters are often ambivalent about their own banishment. For Gregor, his bedroom, to which he is constantly banished by his family, alternately represents both cell and sanctuary, for example. Paralleling Gregor's banishment in the novella is the eventual banishment of the three bearded lodgers. They represent, Sparks says, a further metamorphosis and multiplication of Gregor himself and compound his self-punishment as he watches them overrun the Samsa home.

People are always being banished in Kafka—they are banished from the dinner table, sent off to their bedrooms, set out onto balconies . . . they are transported to penal colonies, exiled to St Petersburg, or even packed off to America. The following short passage from Kafka's *Dearest Father* is a complete exile in miniature.

> I remember one thing from the first years. Perhaps you remember it, too. One night I kept whining for a glass of water —not because I was really thirsty, but more probably out of a desire to annoy others and entertain myself. After a few strong threats went unheeded, you came in, lifted me out of bed, carried me out onto the balcony and left me there for a while, standing in my night shirt before the closed door. I won't say that this wasn't right, for perhaps there was no other way to re-establish peace and quiet, but I will use this incident as an example of your teaching methods and their effect on me. I was tractable enough after that, but I also carried a scar from it. Somehow I could never reconcile the two:

From "Kafka's *Metamorphosis:* On Banishing the Lodgers," by Kimberly Sparks, *Journal of European Studies*, vol. 3, (1973), pp. 230–40. Reprinted by permission of the author.

I could never really connect the commonplace of needlessly asking for water with the extraordinary terror of being carried outside. And for years afterward I was tortured by the thought that this gigantic man, my father, the ultimate authority, could come in the night, for no apparent reason, and carry me from my bed and set me outside; that I was such a nonentity for him.

This is a pathetic banishment and its pathos derives from the poignancy of the remembrance for Kafka. The setting—night, bed, the nameless dark of outside—is appropriate to infant anxiety, and the giant banisher is appropriate to the setting. I am moved by this passage, even though I hear a note of self-indulgence in it. I am affected by the terror of that one night dissolving into the everynight fear of its recurrence.

But I confess that I would be less moved if Kafka had been triplets; I would find it difficult to identify with three close-harmony squallers and my tears cannot rise to the image of three synchronized tots standing on the balcony in identical nightshirts. For when the victim is multiplied, I am released from his claim on my feelings: what was once unique and pathetic has now become a burlesque routine. And of course this is exactly what Kafka does: this is precisely the tone of the banishment of the three bearded lodgers at the end of *The Metamorphosis*.

The principle of multiplication is particularly useful when it comes to expulsions and exiles. By doubling or tripling a character Kafka solves the problem of how to banish him while still keeping him at home. This is of great importance to Kafka, for all of his characters are as deeply ambivalent toward their own exiles as they are towards their origins; they constantly confuse banishment with asylum—and the confusion is easy. Think of Gregor Samsa's bedroom in *The Metamorphosis*, where the distinction between cell and sanctuary is constantly blurred. . . .

THE THREE LODGERS

The entrance of the three lodgers is carefully prepared, and they are tightly bound to the story's entire stock of motifs, themes, images, and gestures. It is through them that Gregor's metamorphosis is recapitulated and raised, once and for all, to burlesque myth. They are the ultimate expression of Kafka's obsession with ceremony and symmetry. In short, the three lodgers are a further metamorphosis and multiplication of Gregor himself.

With the entrance of the three lodgers Gregor becomes a spectator at a puppet show which summarizes all of the action so far. What he is watching, namely, is the visitation of an alien, monstrous presence on his family. Even the brown beetle Gregor is scarcely more burdensome and importunate, scarcely more foreign than these three black 'Chassidim', as Heinz Politzer once called them. And it is a compounding of Gregor's self-punishment that he must look on as the three lodgers usurp the paternal chair, conquer the paternal table, devour with great appetite the food that mother and sister prepare, and finally, let themselves be toadied to by a servile father. But of course he cannot watch the end of the drama—how the father, once again vigorous and dominant in his own house, evicts the three lodgers. He cannot watch because he is dead. This masterpiece of dream-theatre forms the third act of an action which reaches its climax in the terrible apple-throwing scene at the end of Part Two of the story.

There is a certain stillness at the beginning of Part Three, an ominous stillness to be sure: father, mother, and sister recognize that 'family duty requires the suppression of disgust and the exercise of patience, nothing but patience'. It is in this lull that the stage is cleared and reset for the entrance of the three boarders. The living room is transformed, quite literally, into a stage, and Gregor's room, with its door now left open, becomes a darkened loge:

> . . . in his own opinion he was sufficiently compensated for the worsening of his condition by the fact that towards evening the living-room door, which he used to watch intently for an hour or two beforehand, was always thrown open, so that lying in the darkness of his room, invisible to the family, he could see them all at the lamp-lit table and listen to their talk, by general consent, as it were, very different from his earlier eavesdropping.

Now there begins a complicated set of variations on the first part of the novella. The roles of the players are shifted in an uncanny game of musical chairs. Now it is the father, not Gregor, who has to get up at six to go to work. Next Grete has to be freed for the coming scene, and she is in fact replaced by an eerie counter-figure, 'a gigantic bony charwoman with white hair flying round her head'. This transfer of roles is underscored by a transfer of ceremonial paraphernalia, specifically, the broom which has been Grete's badge of office. Kafka uses an ambiguous German word for both sister and the charwoman: *Wärterin*. It is something like the English word 'attendant', which carries the double sense of 'nurse' and 'keeper'. And the broom itself embodies this double meaning. It symbolizes on one hand, Grete's *contact* with Gregor, her caring for him . . . while, on the other hand, it symbolizes the distance she maintains, for she uses the broom to avoid touching Gregor's food with her own hands. In the charwoman's hands the broom becomes an animal prod. But this double meaning of the broom, like the double meaning of 'attendant', should not really surprise us. The difference between nurse and keeper has always been confused in Gregor's mind: in Part One of the story, when Grete and the serving girl are sent out to fetch the locksmith, we learn that Gregor 'hopes for great and remarkable results from both the doctor and the locksmith, without really distinguishing precisely between them'.

In further preparation for the impending spectacle of the three lodgers, there is a fast, economical summation and recapitulation of all of Gregor's previous relationships:

> . . . once more, after this long interval, there appeared in his thoughts the figures of the chief and the chief clerk, the commercial travelers and the apprentices, the porter who was so dull-witted, two or three friends in other firms, a chambermaid in one of the rural hotels, a sweet and fleeting memory, a cashier in a milliner's shop, whom he had wooed earnestly but too slowly—they all appeared, together with strangers or people whom he had quite forgotten, but instead of helping him and his family they were one and all unapproachable and he was glad when they vanished.

And vanish they do—forever. These figures are removed completely from the story, again in preparation for the entrance of the three lodgers.

And just at the moment when Gregor is 'eating hardly anything', the three are suddenly there before us. And they have materialized without complicity, or so it would seem. Kafka introduces them with a gesture very typical of him. He brings them onstage in a kind of throwaway clause tacked on to the end of a sentence. It works the same in English as in German: 'It had become a habit in the family to push into his room things there was no room for elsewhere . . . since one of the rooms had been let to three lodgers'. And the fact that the lodgers are settled in Grete's room—a fact which has great meaning for the interpretation of the story—we learn much later, again in a throwaway line.

But now Gregor, who has never really been able to understand his miserable condition or the confusion of his feelings, is confronted by the complete register of characters for the third act. And what is strange is that in this third act, with the exception of Gregor and his family, we will meet only new characters; characters introduced only for this play within a play. Stranger still, none of them has a name. It is of course clear from the beginning that Gregor does not recognize the three bearded boarders as an extension of himself. How should he? For first of all, as Benno von Wiese points out, their very three-ness make them somehow impersonal, un-individual. And as Wilhelm Emrich puts it, Gregor's own insides are alien to him, so how should he recognize them when they are made external? But it is clear that we are dealing here with just that, Gregor's insides made external; it is the externalization of Gregor's self, his condition, and above all it is the externalization of Gregor's effect on his family . . . or his imagined effect on them. There is even a kind of humour attached to the synchronized behaviour of these three grotesque puppets—gallows humour to be sure. But Gregor will not have Sancho Panza's luck in exorcizing his demon.

A BURLESQUE SELF-CARICATURE

In introducing the lodgers, Kafka quickly binds them to all of the themes and images that we have met thus far in the story:

> These serious gentlemen—all three of them with full beards, as Gregor once observed through a crack in the door—had a passion for order, not only in their own room but, since they were now members of the household, in all its arrangements, especially in the kitchen.

Very strange lodgers indeed! Even their beards are suggestive. Not only do they serve as masks and signs of an almost burlesque authority, but they are an oblique continuation of the animal motif we see in Gregor himself, in the fur-clad woman in the photograph, and in the antenna-like ostrich feather which waves atop the charwoman's hat as she leaves the apartment for the last time. It is through the lodgers that Gregor's obsession with food and eating is sustained and even developed further, while their compulsive fastidiousness is contrasted with the growing disorder in Gregor's room.

Now the puppet show can begin, and it begins quite stag-
ily with the raising of a curtain:

> . . . on one occasion the charwoman left the door open a little
> and it stayed ajar even when the lodgers came in for supper
> and the lamp was lit. They set themselves at the top end of the
> table where formerly Gregor and his father and mother had
> eaten their meals, unfolded their napkins and took knife and
> fork in hand.

The three lodgers have taken over the Samsa dinner table,
and are seated where Gregor and his father and his mother
once sat. They are sitting at the navel of the whole action, for
this table is the ceremonial centre of the Samsa universe.
And to the former trinity of father, mother and Gregor, Kafka
now opposes the alien trinity of the lodgers. (Strange to say,
Kafka omits to mention Grete here, which leads one to spec-
ulate on the hidden nature of the brother-sister relationship.) But the reader's attention has often been directed toward this table. It is the table that Gregor first sees when he
first leaves his room in Part One. And just before the cata-
strophic apple bombardment at the end of Part Two, Gregor
begins 'to crawl to and fro, over everything, walls, furniture,
and ceiling, and finally in his despair, when the whole room
seemed to be reeling about him, fell down onto the middle
of the big table'. These last are just two examples among
many . . . and we can easily determine that whoever is one
up in the story, whoever has the upperhand, even if temporarily, sits at the table and lets himself be waited on. Thus
it is suspicious that the lodgers, the so-called lodgers, usurp
the dinner table and banish the rest of the family to the
kitchen.

Now comes a mimed catalogue of all the motifs, symbols
and gestures which have heretofore been reserved for Gregor and his family . . . beginning with the ritual of eating.
Mother and sister, laden with steaming serving dishes, enter
from the kitchen, and there occurs something which once
and for all erases doubts about the identity of Gregor and the
lodgers.

> The food steamed with a thick vapor. The lodgers bent over
> the food set before them as if to scrutinize it before eating, in
> fact the man in the middle, who seemed to pass for an au-
> thority with the other two, cut a piece of meat as it lay on the
> dish, obviously to discover if it were tender or should be sent
> back to the kitchen.

The innocuous word 'scrutinize'—*prüfen* is the word

Kafka uses—is a direct and literal play on Gregor's 'scrutinizing' of the assortment of food laid before him by Grete at the beginning of Part Two. Then Gregor watches as his father comes into the room, makes a servile tour around the table, cap in hand, before retiring to the kitchen. It is revealing that Gregor sees his father now as 'liveried', not 'uniformed' as he was during the apple-throwing scene.

It becomes clearer and clearer that through the lodgers Gregor is constructing a self-caricature. Gesture after gesture, image after image swims up out of the past, the newspaper is an example. In this story whoever is sitting at the head of the table has the right to read the newspaper, and the newspaper itself becomes a ceremonial object. Before his metamorphosis Gregor used to 'sit with us at the table and read the newspaper', as we learn from Mrs Samsa in Part One. And shortly after that, when Gregor is leaving his room for the first time, we learn that 'breakfast was the most important meal of the day to Gregor's father, who lingered it out for hours over various newspapers'. And it is armed with a walking stick and a newspaper that Gregor's father drives him back into his room in Part One. It is even a 'large newspaper'. The ritual aspect of reading the newspaper is even more strongly brought out in the second part of the story.

> [Gregor] could see through the crack of the door that the gas was turned on in the living room, but while usually at this time his father made a habit of reading the afternoon newspaper in a loud voice to his mother and occasionally to his sister as well, not a sound was now to be heard. Well, perhaps his father had recently given up this habit of reading aloud, which his sister had mentioned so often in conversation and in her letters.

And it is a piece of coldest irony that Gregor's insect meals are always served on a piece of old newspaper.

But now the reading of the newspaper is transformed into a purely visual, theatrical gesture: 'the lodgers had already finished their supper, the one in the middle had brought out a newspaper and *given the other two a page apiece*, and now they were leaning back at ease reading and smoking' (my italics). Reading, i.e. dispensing, the newspaper is still a sign of authority, one can only do it if one is sitting at the head of the table.

The burlesque externalization of Gregor's past is brought out in other ways . . . through Grete's violin-playing, for instance. Although we learned early on that Grete played the violin, we first hear her actually play here in the presence of the three lodgers. 'On that very evening—during the whole of his time there Gregor could not remember ever having heard the violin—the sound of violin-playing came from the kitchen.'

Why does Grete play just now? By any external logic, the violin-playing would seem very sketchily motivated indeed. And why in the world is she playing the violin in the kitchen? But by the laws of Gregor's insides, the motivation is completely satisfactory. For precisely through his positive reaction to the music and the negative reaction of the lodgers does Gregor's ambivalence find full expression.

BANISHING THE LODGERS

With the violin-playing the scene gains momentum and presses toward a climax. The Samsas are brought in from the kitchen (where we cannot see them) and dispersed around the stage: Grete at her music stand in the middle of the room, the father leaning against a door, and the mother in an armchair off in a corner. Grete begins to play and Gregor, 'covered with dust, fluff and hair and remnants of food', begins to creep toward the music. For the third time Gregor Agonistes leaves his room—magical number three! And neither is it the first time that he leaves his room to be confronted by another version of himself, for when he left his den in Part One he was immediately struck by the image of an earlier, more authoritative Gregor: 'Right opposite Gregor on the wall hung a photograph of himself on military service, as a lieutenant, hand on sword, a carefree smile on his face, inviting one to respect his uniform and military bearing.' And now Gregor sees the three importunate strangers standing 'much too close behind the music stand'.

The music seems to have displeased the three lodgers; they retire to the window, from where they catch sight of Gregor creeping into the room. But wonder of wonders, instead of being horrified by what they see, they actually watch him with interest and amusement.

Suddenly everything is set in motion and there follows the third banishment scene. But this time it is not Gregor who is shooed back into his room—it is the three lodgers. Pressed by Mr Samsa and attended by Grete they retreat toward their room. They resist, however, and at the entrance to the room the middle lodger delivers himself of the following speech, in which he gives notice in terms which correspond exactly to Gregor's deepest resentments:

> 'I beg to announce', said the lodger, lifting one hand and look-ing also at Gregor's mother and sister, 'that because of the dis-gusting conditions prevailing in this household and family'—here he spat on the floor with emphatic brevity—'I give you notice on the spot. Naturally I won't pay a penny for the days I have lived here; on the contrary I shall consider bringing on action for damages against you, based on claims—believe me —that will be easily susceptible of proof.'... On that he seized the door-handle and shut it with a slam.

In this speech are expressed feelings which the conscious Gregor could never have put into words.

The family, especially the parents, is confused and de-pressed by this scene. Only Grete can pull herself together, and this she does with a gesture of undeniable self-assertion: '"My dear parents", said Grete, slapping the table with her hand by way of introduction, "things can't go on like this."' Again the ceremonial table, but now it has become a judge's bench. And Gregor, still lying on the living room floor as if para-lyzed, becomes a mute witness for his own prosecution. Her violent attack is mostly for her father's benefit for Gregor's mother is neutralized by a coughing fit, then she falls asleep in her chair—a grotesque touch.

Grete plays prosecutor, judge and hangman in one. In her indictment she labels Gregor not 'him' but 'it.' And her sen-tence, 'We must get rid of it,' she executes herself:

> Hardly was [Gregor] well inside his room when the door was hastily pushed shut, bolted and locked. The sudden noise in his rear startled him so much that his little legs gave way be-neath him. It was his sister who had shown such haste. She had been standing ready waiting and had made a light spring forward. Gregor had not even heard her coming, and she cried 'At last!' to her parents as she turned the key in the lock.

THE FINAL BANISHMENT

In Part One of the story there were three keys to Gregor's room, one for each of the three doors, and they were all care-fully turned from the inside. Now the door that connects to the living room is locked from the outside. Gregor is fin-ished: there is nothing left but to die ... and this he does just as the tower clock strikes three—again the ritual three, the central number of the novella. The whole story is over, at least this is what the Freudian critic Charles Neider says in his book, *The Frozen Sea.* Neider thinks that there is no artistic reason for continuing the story past Gregor's death. The rest of it, he says, is all Kafka's private malice against his family. But this is where Freudian critics often go wrong. Sensitive as they may be to the psychological dimensions of a story, they are frequently insensitive to its purely mechanical exigencies. The Samsa household must be brought to order. And it is.

One, Gregor is accounted for, but Grete's 'We must get rid of it' applies to the counter-Gregor as well—to the three lodgers. And it also applies to the doubling of Grete herself, the bony charwoman who has become superfluous with Gregor's death. All of these demonic rabbits, who have been conjured up only for Part Three of the story, must be exorcized in a way in keeping with the motifs and themes of the novella.

The door-slamming charwoman discovers Gregor's corpse and proclaims that he has *krepiert*—'crapped out', a word which in German is never applied to anything human. And all of the players muster for a viewing of the body. First, the Samsas in a terrible family tableau: 'The father crossed himself and the three women followed his example'. Then the three remaining Samsas retire to the paternal bedroom. Now the lodgers come into the salon, wondering where their breakfast is, again an echo of Part One, then, escorted by the charwoman, they go into Gregor's room and stand around the corpse, 'their hands in the pockets of their somewhat shabby coats'.

And as the lodgers stand there, all of the actors are brought together on stage for the last banishment. It is the moment of the great eviction, for in Kafka's world, even if you have already given notice, you are evicted just the same:

> At that moment the door of the Samsas' bedroom opened and Mr Samsa appeared in his uniform, his wife on one arm, his daughter on the other. They all looked as if they had been crying; from time to time Grete hid her face on her father's arm. 'Leave my house at once' said Mr Samsa.

Two hostile trinities confront each other—the Samsas *vs* the lodgers—but the lodgers, as their role dictates, can now offer only the most pathetic resistance. Their reason for being lies dead at their feet.

And right here the lodgers, in their grotesque synchronization, take on insect characteristics, for as the middle lodger speaks to Mr Samsa, the other two lodgers 'put their hands behind them and kept rubbing them together'. And as the defeated middle lodger leaves the living room forever, the other two go scuttling after him, 'as if afraid that Mr Samsa might get into the hall before them and cut them off from their leader'.

Then mother, father, and Grete watch as the lodgers take up their walking sticks, put on their hats, bow mutely in unison and wind their way down the long staircase. Only after they are satisfied that the three lodgers are gone for good do they set the rest of their affairs in order. They write three letters of excuse to their three employers, then they discharge the demonic charwoman, who leaves with a last door-slam, her ostrich feather bobbing indignantly.

Exit the three lodgers, Gregor's puppet doubles—or triples—for apart from this function they have no names and no professions.

And with the banishment of the lodgers, . . . the essential symmetries of the novella have been established. These supernumeraries are in fact an essential part of the ceremony, and are to be understood as such. It has been their function to play out Gregor's burdening of the family and his burdening of himself, to transform this state of mind into theatrical gestures. It is through the lodgers that we gain insight into the history of Gregor before the metamorphosis. They recapitulate the whole action from beginning to end; or as they say in Latin, *ab ovo usque ad mala*: from the egg to the apple.

CHAPTER 3

The Psychology of *The Metamorphosis*

Conscious, Preconscious, and Unconscious in *The Metamorphosis*

Jean Jofen

Kafka scholar Jean Jofen, Ph.D., of Baruch College in New York, interprets *The Metamorphosis* on its conscious, preconscious, and unconscious levels. Kafka is conscious of portraying Gregor Samsa's father with a mixture of both power, weakness, and absurdity, to overcome the struggles with his own father and the demands of the capitalistic establishment within his society. On a preconscious level, Jofen explains, various symbols of sickness throughout the work suggest Kafka's fear of dying from tuberculosis, even though Kafka wrote the novella eight years before he actually contracted the disease. Finally, Jofen argues, Kafka's unconscious is revealed in the story through symbols Kafka himself does not understand. Gregor's mother's sexy garments and the surrogate role of the sister suggest an oedipal complex in the story, an unhealthy love for the mother, which may explain the theme of guilt and the need for punishment that runs through much of Kafka's work.

To understand *Metamorphosis*, we need to realize that Kafka does not identify "the abnormal" with "the bad." In a letter to his sister Ottla, he writes on Dec. 28, 1916: "The abnormal is not the worst, for we consider as normal (e.g. the World War) ."

In this paper, I will interpret *Metamorphosis* on three levels: the conscious, the preconscious and the unconscious. The first level includes Kafka's relationship to his father and to his family, as well as his attitude to political, social and religious issues. The second level comprises the fear of an approaching illness and eventual death from tuberculosis. The third level

From "*Metamorphosis*," by Jean Jofen, *American Imago*, vol. 35, no. 4 (1978), pp. 347–55. Copyright © The Johns Hopkins University Press. Reprinted with permission of The Johns Hopkins University Press.

describes the unconscious desires arising from Kafka's deep love for his mother (sister), with the concomitant fear and hatred of the father.

Kafka's relationship to his father is symbolized by the ruthless executioner in *The Penal Colony*. The connection between the father and the court is not accidental since Kafka's father was "Expert at the K.K. Country and Criminal Court." It is the father who wears the uniform in the home even when he sleeps.

Nevertheless, it has been noted by Kafka scholars such as Walter Sokel and Ingeborg Heuel, that the father figures in Kafka's work show a shocking double face, namely: "a mixture of authority, power and dignity on the one hand and senility, weakness and absurdity on the other hand." This outward show of strength combined with inner weakness is manifest in the father's original position vis á vis the lodgers and his relationship to his superiors on the job to whom he must listen (bringing them coffee and lunch), and is evidenced when all three members of the family have to write detailed letters of apology to their superiors even in a case of an absence because of a death in the family.

The portrayal of the father as weak is a futile attempt on Kafka's part to overcome his strong father. In his *Letter to my Father*, Kafka admits: "I have already indicated, that in my writing and other related matters, I have made slight attempts to be independent and to escape with only the smallest success; that these attempts will hardly ever be successful is indicated to me by many things."

Yet, in his work, Kafka accuses his father of complete neglect of the child. The authority figure (the chief clerk) in *Metamorphosis* is hard of hearing. Neither the father nor anyone else can understand what Gregor Samsa is saying. The father drives him away not with words but with a hissing noise. There is no verbal communication between them. . . .

In order to gain approval, the son feels called upon to perform superhuman feats (*The Hunger Artist, The Trapeze Artist*), but even these do not gain him any recognition. In real life, seeking approval from his father, Kafka began working the day after he finished his internship as lawyer and on his first job he had to work 8–10 hours daily, which gave him no time to write. This is reflected in *Metamorphosis*.

If a son sees a father as such a powerful figure, he must view himself as very small in relation to him. Much of the misunderstanding in the interpretation of *Metamorphosis* comes from the fact that the first sentence has been wrongly translated: "Als Gregor Samsa eines Morgens aus unruhigen Träumen erwachte, fand er sich in seinem Bett zu einem ungeheuren Ungeziefer verwandelt." (As Gregor Samsa awoke one morning from uneasy dreams he found himself transformed, in his bed, into a gigantic insect.) The German word 'ungeheuer' does not only mean 'gigantic.' It can be translated as 'monstrous,' 'shocking' and 'frightful'. None of the translations imply large size. As a matter of fact, the internal evidence supports the small size of the animal: a) it fits under the opening of a couch, b) it can be pushed away by a newspaper, c) it is small enough to creep on the ceiling and wall, d) its entire body covers a small picture on the wall, e) when it looks up it sees the soles of the father's shoes, f) it has to creep up on a chair to look out of the window and even then cannot see the opposite wall, g) in death, it is so small that it cannot even be distinguished from a small heap of dirt.

That Gregor Samsa sees himself not larger than a mouse can even be inferred from his identification with Josephine in *Josephine and the Mice Folk*. A mouse loves cheese; Gregor Samsa rejects the milk and likes cheese best of all foods. In the story 'In the Synagogue,' the animal which attaches itself to the curtain of the women's section also seems to be of a small size.

The only way someone with such a small ego can get back at a father who is perceived as all-powerful is to embarrass him. This is exactly what Gregor does. He shows himself always when the father is present. He inconveniences the family by scaring away the cook and appears in front of the chief clerk and in front of the lodgers. Nevertheless, his small size makes him powerless. By giving himself the name Samsa, which is reminiscent of the biblical Samson, who was made powerless by a woman, but prayed for strength which was ultimately granted to him, Gregor assumes a degree of strength which he does not possess in reality.

Thus, on the conscious level, we see the struggle with the all-powerful father, which can be translated into a political stance of fighting the "Establishment." This Kafka did by his criticism of the functioning of the capitalistic system. Kafka embraced socialism and became a member in the "Klub mlad'ych" (Club of the Young). *Metamorphosis* shows that the system has no use for a person who can no longer perform at full capacity and by exaggerating the point that even though an employee has performed extraordinarily well all his life, if he were to come late or not show up for work, he would immediately lose his job. It also magnifies the relationship between the employee and his job by having the chief clerk appear in the employee's house, almost by intuition, even before the employee has been late for one hour, and accusing him of pretending to be ill.

THE PRECONSCIOUS

In the preconscious, the author is only dimly aware of the problem; this will be shown by clearly defined symbols. I aim to show that the preconscious thought in *Metamorphosis* is Kafka's fear of becoming sick and dying of tuberculosis. We know that Kafka first contracted tuberculosis in 1921 and that *Metamorphosis* was written in 1913. Why should this fear of sickness, with its accompanying symbol system, appear as early as 1913? In August 1911, Kafka spent a week in the 'Sanatarium Erlenbach' near Zurich, and in July 1912, he spent 3 weeks in a sanatorium in the Hartz mountains. Only after 1912, does the word 'Angst' (anxiety) begin to appear in his diary. What are the indications of this anxiety in *Metamorphosis*?

Gregor's direct indictment of the father is that he caused his sickness by letting him assume the whole responsibility for the family. Symbolically, it is expressed by the father throwing the apples against his back:

> He was already beginning to feel breathless, just as in his former life his lungs had not been very dependable ... suddenly something lightly flung landed close beside him and rolled before him. It was an apple; a second apple followed immediately ... an apple thrown without much force grazed Gregor's back and glanced off harmlessly. But another following immediately *landed right on his back* and sank in. Gregor wanted to drag himself forward, as if this startling, incredible pain could be left behind him ... the apple went on sticking in his flesh as a visible reminder, since no one ventured to remove it. ... The rotting apple in his back and the inflamed area around it, all covered with soft dust, already hardly troubled him. ...

When the father pushes him back into the room, he is also afraid that the stick in the father's hand might hit him in the back and so he moves backwards without turning around, which causes his movements to slow down and annoy his father tremendously. When he finally reaches his room, he starts bleeding profusely. . . .

The other conscious symbol of sickness which we find in *Metamorphosis* is the hospital which cannot yet be seen by him. Gregor's refusal to have the furniture removed from his room shows his determination not to turn it into a bare hospital room. Kafka writes in his letter of July 1922 to Max Brod: "This causes a terrible fear of death, which must not necessarily express itself as fear of death but can also appear as fear of any change." The mother and sister want to remove everything but the sofa, but he fights them off with all his strength. The alarm clock ticks away the time. . . .

The isolation and especially the fear of contamination, which people who come in contact with those suffering from tuberculosis exhibit, is shown by the fact that the sister opens the window wide as soon as she enters the room and that she only touches the food with a broom "never with her hands" whether Gregor has touched it or not. He is given a bowl exclusively for his own use. Even when he is dead, the housekeeper pushes the body only with a stick so that she should not be contaminated.

Other symptoms of tuberculosis are alluded to by the animal that had an 'armor-plated back' and a cough which did not sound human. A tuberculosis patient has difficulty in breathing. Thus, one of the reasons for his suspension from the ceiling and wall (which occurs also in *The Trapeze Artist*) might be the desire to breathe easier and get purer air. It is possible that Kafka went to see doctors many years before the onset of the illness. The reference to the company doctor in *Metamorphosis*, who considers all sick people to be malingerers, as well as the father's attitude, which is almost identical, leads me to believe that the illness, though feared by him, was diagnosed late. The boarders might represent three doctors who are simply amused by him but not alerted to the sickness. He writes in a letter: "This afternoon I fed goats . . . especially Dr. W., the doctor who treats me, is strongly represented among them. The group of experts which consisted of three Jewish doctors, which I fed this evening, was so satisfied with me, that it hardly permitted itself to be driven away in the evening to be milked."

His tuberculosis was the reason which Kafka gave his fiancée when he broke their engagement.

Symbols of sickness abound in *Metamorphosis* and, in particular, symbols of death from tuberculosis. That Gregor dies of hunger is the most obvious. The housekeeper who enters the home at the onset of the sickness looks like death: ". . . a gigantic *bony* charwoman with white hair flying round her head. . . ." It is the housekeeper who reports his death and buries him. This figure might also have its traces in one of the early memories reported by Kafka: He recalls that the housekeeper took him to school every morning and threatened to tell the teacher how badly he had behaved at home. She never made good her threat but it hung over him his whole life. Of course, after his death, with life beginning anew, the housekeeper (death) is dismissed. Tuberculosis slowly consumes the entire body. This has a bearing on the tremendous anger which Gregor has against those who are able to eat with appetite, such as the boarders. . . .

This interpretation is the hardest, since it reaches deepest into Kafka. The unconscious is revealed in symbols which are not understood by Kafka himself. Basically, it is Kafka's love for the mother. This is reflected in *Metamorphosis* where the mother appears every time either in a nightgown or underwear: "He saw his mother rushing towards his father, leaving one after another behind her, on the floor, her loosened petticoats. . . . Mr. Samsa throwing a blanket over his shoulders, Mrs. Samsa in nothing but her nightgown, in this array they entered Gregor's room."

The sister, in the novel, is a mother surrogate, and when Gregor is rejected by her, he decides to die. The squabble between the mother and sister as to who should clean his room also indicates the feeling that neither of them wants to do it. The only one who did not recoil from him was the charwoman (death).

How does the oedipal love appear? I believe that the mother was unconsciously associated by him with "LAW." Kafka had the Jewish concept of law which was "the Torah." The Torah is the holiest scroll of law kept behind a gate in the Synagogue. In his unconscious, he identifies the mother with this holy object. In this sense, we understand the story, "Before the Law." In *The Trial* the gatekeeper is the father who never will permit him to reach the law. This role of the father as gatekeeper is shown also by the uniform of a porter worn in *Metamorphosis*. Kafka studied Jurisprudence which he never practiced. . . .

In *Metamorphosis*, it is the picture of the woman in furs (a mother figure) which he protects with his whole body from being removed from his room. He is separated from the woman by the cold glass, just as the animal in the synagogue is separated from the woman by a curtain to which it clings all its life. We are told that Gregor spent many hours making the frame for this picture. The picture showed . . . "a lady, with a fur cap on and a fur stole, sitting upright and holding out to the spectator a huge fur muff into which her whole forearm had vanished. . . ."

Throughout the novels, we find the love for the mother as Goddess and harlot: forbidden as Goddess but attainable as harlot. In his own life, Kafka fell in love with the forbidden. Milena (a married woman and not Jewish) and a Swiss girl (also not Jewish). In *The Castle*, Kafka is attracted to Frieda who once belonged to Klamm (father figure)—the owner of the castle—, Mother is castle; 'Schloss' in German also means 'lock'—thus forbidden to the son. Klamm lives in 'Herrenhof.' This was also the name of a coffeehouse in Vienna visited by the literati which was commonly called "Hurenhof" (House of Prostitution). . . .

Throughout Kafka's novels runs a terrible guilt, and a need for punishment. He writes in his diary in 1911: "The happiness consisted in this, that the punishment came, and I welcomed it freely, convinced and happily."

When Kafka learns that he has t.b., he writes to Max Brod: "I search all the time for a reason for my illness since I did not simply contract it myself." Why did the father throw apples at the son? Some critics have connected the apples with the forbidden fruit—the apple in Paradise which represents again the forbidden. In his *Parables and Paradoxes* he speaks of 'Paradise': "We were fashioned to live in Paradise, and Paradise was destined to serve us. . . . We were expelled from Paradise, but Paradise was not destroyed. In a sense our expulsion from Paradise was a stroke of luck, for had we not been expelled, Paradise would have had to be destroyed." If we interpret 'Paradise' as 'The Mother' we again see the Oedipus complex.

The constant references to hunger and fasting are also connected with Jewish mysticism and reflect Chassidic tales which show the expiation of guilt through asceticism. The hunger artist fasted forty days as did Christ when tempted by the Devil. Kafka is atoning for some guilt of which he never becomes fully conscious. Yet, all the atonement does not free him from guilt, symbolized by "Schmutz" (dirt). Both Gregor and the hunger artist die in a pile of dirt. Kafka wrote to Milena: "I am dirty, Milena, extremely dirty, that is why I carry on so much about cleanliness."

Guilt, Family Love, and the Dangers of Dependency in *The Metamorphosis*

Norman Friedman

Norman Friedman is a professor of English at Queens College, New York. His publications include *Rhetoric and Style, Poetry: An Introduction to Its Form and Art,* and *E.E. Cummings: The Art of His Poetry.* Friedman delves into Kafka's personal history to discuss the feelings of guilt that plague so many of his characters. From early childhood, Kafka felt inadequate and lacked self-confidence, especially in regards to his father. For this he felt an enormous amount of guilt, which only became magnified as he became more dependent on his father for support during his illness. In *The Metamorphosis,* Friedman explains, Kafka expresses the paradox of Gregor Samsa needing his family's love while being all too aware of the dangers inherent in dependent relationships.

The basic motif in Franz Kafka's life and work is guilt, and the search for freedom from guilt. Indeed, the circumstances of his biography seem to have conspired in insuring that this would be so.

He was born in 1883 in Prague, Czechoslovakia, which was then part of the old Austrian Empire, a large and ungainly assortment of nationalities and states, run by a vast and intricate bureaucracy. And to make matters worse, he was a Jew, so that his life was even more complex and document-ridden than that of the ordinary citizen. Added to these, he was the shy and withdrawn son of a domineering and successful businessman, and this became the primary fact of Kafka's life. In 1919, when he was thirty-six, he wrote a long "Letter to My Father," in which the meaning of this fact becomes painfully clear. His mother, who was to act as intermediary, returned it undelivered to her son, and nothing more was said about it. But Max Brod, Kafka's friend and biographer, published some parts of it after Kafka's death, and in reading these selections, we can see that Kafka's whole soul was warped from childhood by feelings of inadequacy. He felt, and was made to feel, that he could never measure up to the standard of manhood set by his father, and so he went through life haunted by an endless and unendurable shame. The attempt to come to terms with this shame, to get out from under it, governed the entire course of his career. And this task was made doubly difficult by two more twists of the knife: first, he actually loved his father and remembered their good moments together with nostalgic tenderness; second, he had intelligence enough to see that what was torturing him was completely senseless and irrational, yet he still could not free himself of it.

Here are a few central passages from this letter:

> . . . Courage [he writes to his father], resolution, confidence, joy in one thing or another never lasted if you were opposed to it, or even if your opposition was only to be expected—and it was to be expected in nearly everything I did. In your presence—you are an excellent speaker in matters that concern you—I fell into a halting, stuttering way of speech. Even that was too much for you. Finally I kept still, perhaps from stubborness, at first; then because, facing you, I could neither think nor speak any more. And since you were the one who had really brought me up, this affected me in everything I did.

The result of this upbringing was—and here he quotes at the end of this passage the closing words of his novel, *The Trial*—that "I had lost my self-confidence with you, and exchanged a boundless sense of guilt for it. Remembering this boundlessness, I once wrote fittingly about someone: 'He fears that his feeling of shame may even survive him.'"

The rest of his life, Brod comments, Kafka then reconstructs as a series of attempts to break away from his father's influence. He even planned at one time to call his writings *The Attempt to Escape from Father*, and he says:

> . . . My writing was about you, in it I only poured the grief I could not sigh at your breast. It was a purposely drawn-out parting from you, except that you had forced it on me, while I determined its direction. [And so, too, with his life:] My self-appraisal depended on you much more than on anything else, such as, for instance, an outward success. . . . Where I lived, I was repudiated,

judged, suppressed, and although I tried my utmost to escape elsewhere, it never could amount to anything, because it involved the impossible, something that was, with small exceptions, unattainable for my powers.

He went to the German elementary and secondary schools, and when he was eighteen he went to the Prague University. After a few false starts in literature and then chemistry, he decided to study law, sensing the need for a profession which would not involve him personally, which he could master in a routine way, and therefore at which he could succeed without fear of failure. As he himself explains, in the "Letter":

> . . . The point was to find a profession which would most readily permit me [to be indifferent] without injuring my ego too much. And so law was the obvious choice . . . at any rate this choice showed remarkable foresight on my part. Even as a little boy I had sufficient strong premonitions concerning studies and a profession. From these no salvation was to be expected; I resigned myself to that long ago.

And this course seemed to offer hope of a post where he might at least have some time for himself. He became a Doctor of Law in 1906, and after a short period as a clerk in an insurance office, he obtained a position in the semigovernment office of the "Workers' Accident Insurance Institute for the Kingdom of Bohemia," in Prague in 1908. The work proved to be trying, however, and he found it difficult to live the double life of an official and a writer.

In 1912 he met a girl from Berlin, and they became engaged a few years later, but Kafka could not face up to the consequences of such a decision, and broke off with her several times. He blames this vacillation, too, on his subservience to his father:

> . . . The most important obstacle to marriage [he writes] is the already ineradicable conviction that, in order to preserve and especially to guide a family, all the qualities I see in you are necessary—and I mean all of them, the good and the bad. . . . Of all these qualities I had comparatively few, almost none, in fact. And yet what right had I to risk marriage, seeing, as I did, that you yourself had a hard struggle during your married life that you even failed toward your children.

After the outbreak of World War I, he was exempted from military service as the employee of an office doing essential work. In 1921 he began to have lung trouble, and spent most of his remaining years in sanatariums. He died of tuberculosis in 1924, at the age of forty-one.

Very little of his work was published during his lifetime, and so diffident, so morbidly inadequate did he feel, that before he died he ordered Max Brod to destroy the unfinished manu-scripts of his three great novels, *Amerika, The Trial*, and *The Castle*. Luckily for us, his friend took upon himself the terrible burden of disregarding Kafka's wishes and published these works posthumously.

A SEARCH FOR FREEDOM

The weak son of a strong father; a Jew in a German world; an official in a government bureau; a citizen in a feudal empire; an artist trying to find time to write in the midst of the grinding business of making a living; a modern man whose life was lived in the shadow of two world wars—what sort of vision of life would the writings of such a man reveal? What *could* they reveal? Guilt, and the search for freedom from guilt—Kafka writes, although never directly of current events, of the condition of twentieth-century man. Alone, homeless, and anxiety-ridden; outsiders, exiles, and aliens, Kafka's strange heroes are at once projections of their creator's neurosis and of our own—for he felt in an especially acute form what we all feel in one degree or another. We are in a nightmare world which is all too real, where forces beyond our control or comprehension are massed destructively against us, and where our love never seems to go right. And nowhere can we find whoever or whatever is responsible, for the enemy is so close to us that we cannot see him—he is inside us, he is ourselves. It does not matter whether this leader or that one is in power: the rush of our doom seems to menace us always. So we are sick, sick with fear, shame, and paralysis of the soul. The more we try to do something about it, the more involved we become in the sticky web of defeat and despair.

The world which we find in his books, then, is a world of parable and allegory, a world in which lonely men wander down endless corridors trying to find a way, a door, to the answer of the riddle of their existence, trying to make sense out of a senseless life. They are obstinately rational in the midst of irrationality, and they patiently and desperately and stubbornly go from clerk to official, from office to bureau, in an endless quest to discover what crime they have accused of, who the judges are, and how they can defend themselves. They are faced with an enormously and mysteriously proliferating social structure where those at the bottom do not know who is at the top, or whether anybody is at the top at all. . . .

It is with a shock that we realize that what looks like a nightmare is actually our world. For Kafka is a master of the art of serious fantasy: he treats the fantastic literally, and as a result we can see that the literal world is fantastic. The point is not to provide us with an escape from our world, but rather to bring us closer to it. Starting with some weird and impossible occurrence—as, for example, a man turning into a bug one gray morning—he proceeds soberly and realistically to show how this man feels, how he worries about being late for work, how it is difficult for him to turn his doorknob, how his family is horrified but never incredulous. Beginning, in other words, with a completely unnatural event, he treats it so naturally thereafter that all seems perfectly logical and real. The result is that we soon begin to recognize that exaggeration and distortion are serving a significant artistic function: Kafka sees what is happening to the inner reality of our world—he sees the threats developing beneath the surface of our lives because they are closer to the surface of his life than of ours—and by means of the special catastrophes of fantasy brings them vividly to light, making visible the hidden and known the secret. The exaggerations and distortions are poetic license, but the threats they reveal are palpable; they are there, dwelling within the lives of us all. And so it is that when we return to the "real" world we know, after reading his fables and fancies, we are able to see it more clearly. The real world *is* fantastic, and is becoming more so every day. And so it is that we see that Kafka's fables are not so fabulous after all: we have come full circle, from the real to the fantastic, and back again to the real.

Critics have argued over whether Kafka sees an answer to this enormous puzzle, and if he does, just what that answer is. Does he see any hope, or nothing but despair? Does he believe in God, or in Reason, or in anything? Does he urge the individual to oppose the system, or to join it? Does he see any escape, any freedom? Does he think that life is worthwhile, or not? The fact is that he did not have the decisiveness either to believe or to disbelieve—or perhaps his subtle and ironic attitude was a form of courage. Although readers can find grounds in his work for different conclusions, I believe something *can* be said about his meaning, if that something is inclusive enough. Let us beware of trying to fit such a complex man and artist into any either-or scheme of interpretation: he was as aware of the loneliness of the outsider as he was of the insanity of society, and in *The Metamorphosis*, for example, he is as aware of the need for family love as he is of its dangers. He is saying, in other words, that man needs society, man needs the family, but that he needs to be himself as well. The problem is how to reconcile these different and sometimes opposing needs, and the solution, as I hope to show, has something to do with the courage required for a man to cast off a love which has enslaved him, or which he is using in order to enslave himself. Kafka believes in love, and in freedom from love at one and the same time. This paradox will take some explaining.

But first, let us turn to the story itself:

> . . . As Gregor Samsa awoke one morning from a troubled dream, he found himself changed in his bed to some monstrous kind of vermin.

> . . . He lay on his back, which was as hard as armor plate, and raising his head a little, he could see the arch of his great, brown belly, divided by bowed corrugations. The bed-cover was slipping helplessly off the summit of the curve, and Gregor's legs, pitiably thin, compared with their former size, fluttered helplessly before his eyes.

"What has happened?" he thought. It was no dream. This is a young man who has been supporting his father, mother, and sister for the past four years, as a commercial traveler. His father's business had failed five years ago, and Gregor has five or six more years to go before he will have paid off the money his father owes to his employer. As he wakes up this morning in this strange condition, his first anxiety is about his job. His family knock at his bedroom door, but they cannot get in. The manager of his office is sent to find out why he is not at work, and when the door is finally opened, they all panic when they see him thus changed. Gregor himself cannot quite realize what has happened, for within himself he still feels he is the same. Their horror, therefore, is all the more poignant, as we see it from his point of view. The first section of the story ends with his father's beating him back into his room.

From this point on, both he and his family begin to change––they for the better, he for the worse, so that the story is built on something of an hourglass pattern. Up to this point, they have been his parasites and had fallen into a psychosomatic torpor as a result of their dependence on him. The father is "an old man who had ceased to work five years before," and this had been "his first holiday in a life entirely devoted to work and unsuccess." He "had become very fat and moved with great difficulty. And the old mother . . . passed a good deal of her time each day lying on the sofa, panting and wheezing under the open window." The sister, finally, "only" seventeen years old, was well "suited to the life she had led . . . nicely dressed, getting plenty of sleep, helping in the house, taking part in a few harmless little entertainments, and playing her violin."

The point is that it is out of the anguish of their horror and their need to support themselves that they begin freeing themselves from their dependency upon Gregor. Indeed, the title may refer as much to their change as to his. The father gets a job, and his appearance improves: "his white hair, ordinarily untidy, had been carefully brushed till it shone." The mother does needlework at home for a lingerie shop, "and the sister, who had obtained a job as a shop assistant, would study shorthand or French in hope of improving her position." At the end we read: "On a careful reflection, they decided that things were not nearly so bad as they might have been, for—and this was a point they had not hitherto realized—they had all three found really interesting occupations which looked even more promising in the future."

In the meantime, Gregor becomes in turn *their* parasite, and in a very literal form. His room has to be cleared to allow him space to move about in, and moldy food has to be shoved into it to appease his bug-like appetite. He still has some human feelings left, however, and yearns for care and company. One night he wanders out into the dining room and his father has to bombard him with apples in order to drive him back into his room. One of them lodges in his back and festers there. So ends the second part.

With the third and last part, the opposing changes in this double plot come to their logical conclusions. In order to bring in some more money, the family have taken in three men as boarders, but the presence of this monster, who was once their son and brother, in the house is a continuing cause of discomfort and despair. They do not know what to do with him. Even the sister, who has been the kindest of all to him, now wants to get rid of this bug which is ruining their lives. Gregor, who has become weakened as a result of the wound and the subsequent loss of his appetite, and who has had difficulty in retaining his human feelings anyway, simply retreats to his by now filthy room and passes quietly away. . . .

Some time later, free at last, his family take an excursion to the country. And the story ends on this hopeful note:

Herr and Frau Samsa noticed almost together that, during this affair, Grete had blossomed into a fine strapping girl, despite the make-up which made her cheeks look pale. They became calmer; almost unconsciously they exchanged glances; it occurred to both of them that it would soon be time for her to find a husband. And it seemed to them that their daughter's gestures were a confirmation of these new dreams of theirs, an encouragement for their good intentions, when, at the end of the journey, the girl rose before them and stretched her young body.

What can the implications of such a story be? It is, as I have already suggested, about family love and the dangers of dependency in such a situation. In the beginning, the family has been Gregor's parasite, and then he becomes theirs. Two harmful consequences are involved in this sort of love: the dependent one becomes weak, and the strong one becomes paradoxically entrapped in his responsibilities toward the weak one. Thus, before his change, Gregor's family had fallen into a useless stupor, and he had become enslaved by the endless task of paying off his father's debts and supporting the family—he had no normal life of his own, and his growth was as effectively blocked as theirs. After his change, the tables were turned, and he becomes dependent while they become chained to the hopeless responsibility of taking care of him. A way out of this vicious circle must be found, however, and his death frees them finally to live and grow again.

The story says, in other words, that we must be free of the dependency of love in order to be ourselves. This statement does not mean that we must be *free* of love, but of the *dependency* of love. We might say that love is provisional rather than absolute, and that when one person becomes so dependent upon the love of another that he prevents the other's growth, as well as his own, then both must free themselves of such a love. Just as his growth is thwarted by their dependency, so too is theirs blocked when he becomes dependent on them. And just as his family were not fulfilling their capacities when they were his parasites, so too was he becoming less than himself when he was their parasite. As his sister says: "I will not mention my brother's name when I speak of this monster here; I merely want to say: we must find some means of getting rid of it. We have done all that is humanly possible to care for it, to put up with it; I believe that nobody could reproach us in the least." And so it is that misfortune, in a paradoxical way, can sometimes free us from a love we cannot break away from on our own and so allow us to become ourselves: he must become a bug in order to release them from their dependency on him, and he must die in order to allow them to grow. Through this involuntary exchange of roles, he redeems them.

But it is a tragic redemption. Gregor still has a few human feelings left at the end, and we feel that his sacrifice is a cruel price to pay for his family's welfare. Especially since they are somewhat shallow people, and even in their renewed vitality at the end, they seem somewhat coarse and vulgar. But what, after all, were the alternatives? Had he continued on as the sole support of his family, neither he nor they would have benefitted. For he was not really alive at all in his role as provider, and ironically his continued success in that very role could only have reduced his family further in their moral degradation. Even if he had paid off that impossible debt, they all would have lost in the end—he wasted by overwork and they wallowing in indolence. As it turns out, he paid off the debt in a better way after all.

A CAREER OF FAILURE

We may ask, finally, how these implications relate to what we have been saying about Kafka's life and vision. We have come, in our discussion, from the projection of his family problems into a social vision, back to a concern with family life itself, the root and source of that vision. Only something has gotten turned around in the process, for the personal situation has been reversed: in this story, at least to begin with, it is the father who is weak and the son who is strong, and it is the family which must be freed from the son rather than the son from the family. This reversal of roles makes the issue more universal and less personal, and it makes it less stereotyped by showing that the dependency problem works both ways. It is an artistic tour de force thus to turn the son's inadequacy into the family's. Of course the story itself, in detailing Gregor's change from breadwinner to parasite, reverses these roles once again, and thus does reflect more immediately Kafka's personal sense of inadequacy, his sense of being indeed a bug, and his feeling that it would be better for all concerned if he did die.

I remarked earlier that Kafka not only feared his father, but he loved him as well. He writes in his "Letter":

> . . . when I used to see you, tired out on those hot summer noons, taking a nap after lunch in your store, your elbow stemmed on the desk; or on Summer Sundays, when you arrived exhausted on a visit to your family in the country; or the time when mother was seriously ill, when you leaned against the bookcase, shaking with sobs; or during my recent illness, when you came softly into my room, remaining on the threshold and stretching your neck to see me in bed, and then, out of consideration, greeting me only with a wave of your hand. At such times I would lie down and cry with happiness, and I am crying again while writing it down.

But it is as if he were saying in this story that only by freeing himself from this love could he become free of this fear.

In his life, however, he could not manage such freedom, for he could not find it in himself to reject his father as Gregor's family had to reject him, perhaps because he could not see his father as a revolting insect—only himself. In his letter, he puts these imagined words of reproach against the son in his father's mouth:

> . . . . You have simply made up your mind to live entirely on me. I admit that we are fighting each other, but there are two kinds of fight. There is the knightly battle, where equal opponents are pitted against each other, each for himself, each loses for himself or wins for himself. And there is the struggle of vermin, which not only stings, but at the same time preserves itself by sucking the other's blood . . . such are you. You are not fit for life, but in order to live in comfort, without worry or self-reproach, you prove that I have taken away your fitness for life and put it all into my pocket.

Max Brod speculates that this is a crucial passage for the understanding of *The Metamorphosis*, and I think he is right.

It was the tragedy of Kafka's life that he could see the way to freedom, but could not bring himself to take it. Although he wanted desperately to free himself from his dependency on his father, he could not surrender the comfort of his love for his father, a love which enslaved him because it enabled him, in a twisted and neurotic way, to avoid self-reproach for his inadequacies, inadequacies of which he was somewhat too exquisitely aware and on whose bitter fruit he had to feed in order to live at all. By thus convicting himself of defeat in advance, he simply did not have to try to succeed, for if he tried and then failed, he would have had only himself to blame. To try is to put one's efforts to the test of experience, and this Kafka could not risk, for then the failure would be his and not his father's at all. That is why he purposely sought out a dull profession, that is why he could not marry, and that is why he wanted his manuscripts burned after his death. He made a career out of failure by refusing to risk success.

But he also made great art out of it, so that in a paradoxical way he succeeded after all. What he could see but not act upon as a man, he could, as a writer, have his characters both realize and do something about. In this way, he has left us the legacy of a partial victory at least. By making a fantasy out of the problem of family love, and then by treating the fantasy as real, he has shown us that the inner reality *is* fantastic indeed. The metamorphosis of a man into an insect symbolizes parasitism: Gregor becomes literally what his family had become figuratively––a vermin, a creature which not only stings, but which at the same time preserves itself by sucking the other's blood.

How can such parasitism be explained? If someone does not approve of you, he can make you feel inadequate only if you want his approval, only if you care about his opinion. Now this wanting and caring can be motivated either by your fear of him or your love for him, or by a mixture of both. Your fear may be caused by some power he has over you, and your love by some tenderness he has shown toward you or by your sense of duty toward him. Obviously, the parent-child relationship has a great potential for producing love and fear: this is what happened to Kafka in relation to his father, and this is what happens, in a reverse way, to Gregor's family in relation to Gregor.

The point is that this caring, which enables you to nourish your feelings of inadequacy instead of seeing that the other's love may be at fault, may be a cover-up for your fear of failure, for it allows you covertly to make the person you love responsible for your own inadequacies. Your love for him has made his smiles or frowns the cause of your joys and despairs. If you did not care about his approval, you would not be able to feel he was responsible when you feel you have failed. The attribution of responsibility is the vermin's sting, and the love is the bloodsucking of the parasite—the love which makes your whole emotional life dependent on him, and which in turn allows you to hold him responsible in the first place. Thus does your dependency become a form of domination, and thus does the person you have placed in the commanding role become your prisoner, the prisoner of his victim. For you are asking him to give you what no one can give you except yourself: security, self-confidence, and self-esteem. Your success or failure depends on his approval or disapproval, and so is not a knightly battle where "each loses for himself or wins for himself." That is why it is a dependent love, and that is why such a love is wrong: it allows you "to live in comfort, without worry or self-reproach." When you cannot win security and self-esteem by trying something on your own, this love becomes a substitute for independent risk taking and so prevents you from growing. The answer is easy to see but hard to do: you must free yourself from this love in order to become yourself; you must cease to care about the person who has reduced you—whether because of your fear or your love—to ineffectuality; you must purge yourself of your concern for him.

That is why Kafka had Gregor turn into a bug: so that his family would be able to stop caring about him. Once they see that he is no longer their son and brother, they no longer feel responsible for loving him and so are free to grow and prosper for themselves. It is almost as if Gregor, in seeing that they had become his helpless parasites, decided unconsciously to exchange places with them in order to free them, for they could not find it in themselves to break away from their dependency on him any more than Kafka could find it in himself to break away from his dependency on his father. Thus he made himself their dependent, becoming the bug in fact that they were becoming figuratively, so that they could no longer depend on him even if they wanted to. They are forced by his subservience to become independent, but they must also stop loving him in order to stand on their own feet. And they cannot love a bug—no one can—so they are free.

His support of them was ruining them all anyway—it is as if he chose to sacrifice himself quickly rather than drag the ordeal out endlessly. In this way, they can be free of him, and do it without guilt in the bargain. They would have earned from us even less sympathy than they do now if they had rejected him when he was still in human form: his metamorphosis enables them to do what they otherwise could not have done. His change is therefore, from their point of view, ultimately an act of mercy, for it lets them off the hook, as it were. The worm has indeed turned, or rather the strong one has made himself weak in order to make the weak ones strong. They must do to him what he was unable to do to them; unable to quit them, he makes them quit him. They cannot lift themselves by their bootstraps. As the parasites, they must stop loving him, but they cannot do so until he is the bug. A parasite is by nature dependent, and can only rebel when the one he is feeding on starts feeding on him. There is a delayed reaction here, for Kafka understood that once a parasite, always a parasite, that a vermin cannot will his own freedom: he has to be vanquished and then freed by another vermin, not a knight. Had Kafka's father become hopelessly sick or crippled, Kafka might have been freed from his bug-hood. But Kafka was the one who got tuberculosis instead, and died, imprisoned by love to the end.

The Roach's Cold Feet: Bachelor Panic in *The Metamorphosis*

James M. McGlathery

Kafka scholar James M. McGlathery of the University of Illinois contends that Gregor Samsa's metamorphosis represents his yearning for sexual innocence and his guilt regarding his lack of desire for sex and marriage. Rather than marry one of a couple of minor love interests in his life, Gregor is eager to take over his father's role as breadwinner for his family. After he has safely escaped the altar in this manner, and after his metamorphosis, however, Gregor rivals his father for the affection of his mother and sister, as he begins to harbor erotic feelings for both of them. In this light, Gregor is a sexual coward, having turned his role of brother and protector of his family into a substitute role of husband.

At least since the important studies by Heinz Politzer (1962) and Walter Sokel (1964), it has become generally accepted that the blossoming of Kafka's writing career not only coincided with his engagement to Felice Bauer, but that the two developments were intimately related. Thus, those critics who prefer to deemphasize the role of erotic feeling in Kafka's works must recognize that the burden of proof lies with them. It is another question, of course, just what this eroticism means and how it is intended. To be sure, Kafka's diaries tell us much concerning his feelings about sexuality as he contemplated marriage, but diaries and literary works are not the same thing, even in the extreme case where the work in question is a memoir, not merely a heavily autobiographical piece. Kafka's tales, of course, are indeed personal confessions, yet done with considerable self-irony, to the point where self is subordinated to the

From "Desire's Persecutions in Kafka's *Judgment, Metamorphosis*, and *A Country Doctor*," by James M. McGlathery, *Perspectives on Contemporary Literature*, vol. 7 (1981), pp. 54–63. Reprinted by permission of the University Press of Kentucky.

demands of art. The element of self-irony is all the greater be-cause in many respects Kafka was writing in the comic vein, even though his tales typically end with the central figure's death. The point therefore needs to be made that, while Politzer, Sokel, and others have devoted some attention to the role of erotic psychology in Kafka's stories, the possibility has been overlooked that in his tales . . . Kafka may be offering us self-ironic, comic portrayals of his bachelor panic over the thought of marrying.

In . . . "The Metamorphosis," . . . Gregor Samsa labors un-der something akin to persecution or oppression . . . under his transformation into an insect. . . . Gregor's reactions to his plight are in many respects irrational, and there is even reason to believe that the adventure, which is told largely from his point of view, is not only fantastic but indeed amounts to fan-tasy on his part. This lack of recognition, and hence self-deception, is reminiscent of the comic tradition, in which the clown is often shown to be laboring under an emotionally produced misapprehension of his situation, viewed objec-tively. Even more important, with regard to the essentially comic situation . . . is that the fantastic adventure experienced by Gregor as being real is not only imaginary, but also likely a substitute for the actual object of his panic, that is, marriage and its physical consummation. A case can be made for con-tending that in this story, as modern as it is in many respects, the older comic type of the bachelor on the run from "Desire's persecutions" has enjoyed a rebirth. . . .

GREGOR'S YEARNING FOR SEXUAL INNOCENCE

If Georg Bendemann in "The Judgment" likely dies a sexual coward, what about Gregor Samsa in "The Metamorphosis," whose problems do not seem, at least, to be primarily of an erotic nature? One thing is obvious enough. Gregor's belief that he has been transformed into an insect belongs clearly to the realm of fantasy. . . . The question then is whether this dras-tic fantasy is motivated perhaps to an even greater extent by unadmitted feelings of guilt regarding sex and marriage.

. . . Gregor does not even have a girl friend, and his one or two romantic involvements appear to have been abortive. . . . Gregor is seemingly a "wallflower," the sort of young man who would seem sooner to be persecuted by doubt that a woman would ever marry him, than by irrational, unconscious panic about the wedding night. And yet Desire's persecutions do seem to play a key role in motivating Gregor's flight into fantasy. As an insect, Gregor has a rationalization for his celibacy, regardless of whether the latter is a voluntary or an involuntary condition. The metamorphosis also makes possible Gregor's return to something like the role of a child, so that one may suspect that . . . Gregor's imaginary transformation is produced by a yearning for the sexual innocence and impotence of his boyhood. Behind the relatively obvious urge to regress lies Gregor's largely unadmitted bachelor panic about the need to prove his manhood, and his fantasies are a projection of this sexual guilt.

There has been considerable attention paid by critics to erotic elements in "The Metamorphosis," but the story's point has almost always been found to lie elsewhere. Wilhelm Emrich argued that Gregor's metamorphosis "concerned the 'unknown nourishment,' which cannot be found on earth," and that it was meant "to awaken in him the 'longing' for this 'nourishment.'" Heinz Politzer carried this argument a step farther by asking whether Gregor's guilt did not "consist in his inability to reach beyond himself, in his desire to grasp and digest the 'unknown nourishment,'" although Politzer then made the disclaimer that "We would moralize unduly if we assumed that his preoccupation with the material side of life has caused his metamorphosis. . . ." Meanwhile, Walter Sokel did give considerable weight to the erotic element in Gregor's motivations, making such points as that "the metamorphosis puts him in a position in which all women have to look down on him repulsively, inimically, disgustedly—even physically." But Sokel's perspective is largely that of Freudian critics, as for example where he finds that in Gregor's case "The love relationship with women is primarily a weapon in the hero's struggle with the man in authority," and that "In Georg Bendemann and Gregor Samsa . . . , Kafka created characters who had tried to rival and succeed their fathers, failed in the attempt, and were horribly punished."

Gregor's unadmitted, unconscious sexual guilt likely concerns his having escaped the altar by seizing the opportunity to replace his father as the family's provider, when Samsa Sr. failed in business. Sexual rivalry with the father certainly was a motivating factor in Gregor's eagerness to assume the role of provider. When we first see Gregor, however, it is precisely that role as provider which has turned sour, to the point where Gregor has come to resent not only his salesman's job, but what he now feels to be exploitation of him by the family. The feeling that ultimately produces Gregor's "metamorphosis," however, may be his suppressed guilt that, while the family may be materially dependent on him, he is emotionally dependent on them to a degree and in ways that are inappropriate for a man of his age. Gregor long since should have established a household and family of his own; instead he has seized an opportunity for rationalizing his continued emotional parasitism in the bosom of the family. In terms of sexual roles, Gregor likely suffers from suppressed awareness that, precisely in his heroic sacrifice for the family, he is, as the English saying goes, "not a man, but a mouse," or rather a parasitic insect. Thus, the nature of his guilt is projected in the form he assumes in his imaginary metamorphosis.

BACHELOR GUILT

Perhaps the best evidence that Gregor suffers from bachelor guilt is the mention toward the story's end (beginning of the third, and last, section) of "a chambermaid from a hotel in the provinces, a dear, fleeting memory, [and] a cashieress in a hat store whom he had courted seriously, but too slowly." These two erotic interests are mentioned among the people who pass through Gregor's mind as he momentarily contemplates taking "the family's affairs in hand again, just as before," yet Gregor finds that the two women, together with the people at his work, "instead of helping him and his family, were all inaccessible." The reason for this inaccessibility is obviously that since Gregor is now an insect—or rather, insane—these bridges have been burned. Yet burning those bridges likely was the motivation for his fantasy in the first place, and, most important, his flight from his job is now brought into association with his failure to marry, that is, with his unadmitted, panicked flight from Desire.

The question of Gregor's feelings about the opposite sex is raised, indeed, at the story's outset, if only implicitly. It is reported that Gregor had cut out the picture of a woman in furs from an illustrated magazine, made a gold frame for it, and hung it in his room. The woman obviously represents for Gregor what American soldiers in World War II were to call a "pin-up," a beloved dream whom, though her existence was real enough, one had really no hope of meeting, much less marrying. Gregor's elegantly dressed "pin-up," however, cannot be an object of erotic fantasizing in the pornographic sense. Indeed, she is also a far cry from the chambermaid and the cashieress, with whom he had become involved; thus, she doubtless represents a thoroughly unrealistic dream for Gregor of marrying above, not below his station—and a beautiful celebrity at that! For a bachelor unconsciously on the run from Desire's persecutions, such love from afar serves as a safe infatuation.

While Gregor can hardly harbor any hope of involvement with the woman in the picture, as the family's bachelor son he does enjoy the ministrations of his mother and sister. He is clearly jealous of their affection and perceives his father as a rival in this regard. At the same time, Gregor evidently still needs the dream of a potential erotic involvement outside the family, and thus he moves decisively to prevent the removal of the woman's picture, after the mother and sister have decided to clear his room of its furnishings. It may be, however, that fear of the picture's removal merely projects Gregor's bachelor guilt: the picture's function has been perhaps to maintain his self-delusion that the mother and sister are not the true objects of his yearning, although it is clear that he dreams of the women in his family in the role of angels of his rescue and comfort.

That an Oedipus complex in the strictest sense is not Gregor's underlying problem is indicated by the fact that his feelings toward the sister are even more intense than those toward the mother; at least, his feelings toward Grete are the more erotic and incestuous. Gregor's sexual cowardice appears to consist chiefly in having made the role of older brother, as protector and benefactor of a younger sister, a substitute for the role of husband. Proving himself a hero in his parents' eyes thus may have been less important to him than appearing so to Grete. What Gregor regrets most intensely about having lost his job as a result of his "transformation" is that he will not be able to fulfill his dream of sending the sister to study violin at a conservatory. Most telling is Gregor's gnomish fantasy about getting the sister to come into his room to play the violin for him—a fantasy excused by his wish to rescue Grete from the impoliteness of the borders whom the family has had to take in since Gregor ceased being the provider. In this fantasy Gregor appears as though a little boy, a younger brother who jealously yearns to be rewarded for his role as protector and benefactor by being allowed to kiss the sister on the neck. Here Gregor reveals the deepest secret regarding his sexual guilt, and thereby the ultimate reason why he believes that he has been transformed into an insect. He unconsciously has attempted to make the sister so dependent on him—to "wed" her to himself materially and, as far as possible, emotionally—so that she would not marry and that he would not have to marry.

When the story is read in this light, it is no mystery why Gregor's death not only is felt by the sister to be a liberation, but also makes her parents suddenly realize that she "had blossomed into a beautiful and voluptuous maiden." As though overnight, she has become ripe for marriage. Not simply the burden of Gregor's transformation or madness, but even more the emotional problem that had produced it, kept the sister emotionally in a state of arrested development, in a prepubescent stage of devotion to an older sibling of the opposite sex. With the brother's death, however, the spell has ended. And whether this scene is viewed as belonging to Gregor's fantasy or to reality, the point remains essentially the same.

CHAPTER 4

Interpretive Criticism About *The Metamorphosis*

Revolt Against the Dehumanized World

Alexander Taylor

A Ph.D. candidate at the University of Connecticut, Alexander Taylor teaches American Studies at University High School in Storrs, Connecticut. He has published numerous poems and articles in *The Massachusetts Review, Fiddlehead,* and other literary journals. Taylor defines Gregor's transformation in *The Metamorphosis* as his revolt against his dehumanizing world. Gregor does not know how to fulfill himself and express love among those who are both unsympathetic and violent toward him, revolted by the physical changes that have come over him. As an outcast, Gregor revolts further, denying the mechanized and empty world of public order, until realizing that he is unable to live in such an atmosphere of complete rejection.

Perhaps the failing of some of the Kafka criticism is the attempt to clarify something that should remain a riddle. *Metamorphosis* has certainly had multiple interpretations, many of them prompted by the temptation to lay the corpus of Kafka's works neatly on the psychoanalyst's couch, thus viewing the story as an exercise in masochism or a session in therapy. However, it seems to me that if we look at the story from the viewpoint that it is not Gregor who is sick, but his environment, we will see the story as the reaction of a perceptive individual against a dehumanizing world of order, within which most people are enslaved. For instance, consider Gregor's thoughts as he hears the family lamenting the impossibility of moving to another apartment because of the problem of moving him in his transformed state:

> Yet Gregor saw well enough that consideration for him was not the main difficulty preventing the removal, for they could easily have shifted him in some suitable box with a few air holes in it. What really kept them from moving into another flat was

From "The Waking: The Theme of Kafka's *Metamorphosis*," by Alexander Taylor, *Studies in Short Fiction*, vol. 2, no. 4 (1965), pp. 337–42. Reprinted with permission of *Studies in Short Fiction.*

rather their own complete hopelessness and the belief that they had been singled out for misfortune such as had never happened to any of their relations or acquaintances. They fulfilled to the uttermost all that the world demands of poor people. The father fetched breakfast for the small clerks in the bank; the mother devoted her energies to making underwear for strangers; the sister trotted to and fro behind the counters at the behest of customers. But more than this they had not the strength to do.

Another indication of the dehumanized world is the father's wearing his bank messenger's uniform at home, where it "began to look dirty despite all the loving care of the mother and sister to keep it clean." The world of order carried into the home destroys the possibility of true human love.

The riddle is Gregor's riddle—how to fulfill himself and simultaneously express his love and understanding among people who react unsympathetically, even violently, against his transformation, and who refuse to recognize his ability to understand them, because they can't understand him. Even more is the riddle Gregor's because he does not understand himself.

The story begins with Gregor's waking; it is a waking in more than one sense, and is therefore represented by his transformation to a giant beetle. Gregor's mind at first refuses to accept this condition even though he senses "it was no dream." He thinks, "What about sleeping a little longer and forgetting all this nonsense?" Then his thoughts turn to his job. It is obvious that he intensely dislikes his work as a travelling salesman ("The devil take it all"), but that on the other hand feels duty bound to continue working until he has saved enough money to pay back his parents' debt to the chief.

Other details of his thoughts, the spineless and stupid porter who checks on him and the insurance doctor who considers "all mankind as perfectly healthy malingerers" emphasize the distrust and suspicion surrounding Gregor and his disgust at this state of affairs.

This disgust stems from Gregor's desire to establish I-thou relationships in a world of I-it or I-she or I-he relationships. (I-thou relationships are those of true human affection. I-it are those in which the I uses the person or object as a tool to reach his ends.) In general the people surrounding Gregor do not experience a warm love through a genuine communication, but see each other as objects that are useful or to be used. For instance, the chief clerk is sent to Gregor by the firm because

Gregor is not functioning as an object or tool of the firm. When Gregor's mother says that Gregor must be ill, the clerk answers, "I can't think of any other explanation, madam . . . I hope it's nothing serious. Although on the other hand I must say that we men of business—fortunately or unfortunately—very often simply have to ignore any slight indisposition, since business must be attended to."

Gregor's relationship to his family previous to his transformation had really become an I-it relationship (further emphasized by the fact that the father had money of his own salted away which he did not use to help pay back his own debt, a debt which kept Gregor in bondage to the firm). . . .

Gregor desires desperately to achieve a relation with a "special uprush of warm feeling" but fails to do so in a dehumanized world. It is ironical that his unconscious desire to be his true self destroys his relationship to the two people with whom he most nearly achieved this warm feeling—his mother and his sister.

THE RIDDLE OF HUMAN EXISTENCE

How do we interpret Gregor's transformation? First, we note that in the beginning Gregor does not consciously will the change, and in fact tries to deny it to himself. Second, Gregor is puzzled about his change, and is constantly questioning himself about it (for instance, when he notes that his wounds heal more rapidly, he asks "Am I less sensitive now?"). Third, Gregor yearns passionately for association with the family; he presses his body against the door to catch snatches of family conversation. Fourth, Gregor has always shown almost perverse consideration for the firm and for other members of his family at the expense of his own desires, and immediately after the transformation continues to do so. Fifth, that Gregor, upon waking, is "unusually hungry." And last, Gregor's transformation is a continuing process, initially a retrogression into the natural state of an insect, but later a gradual movement toward self-assertion at the expense of the comfort of others.

The riddle is Gregor's riddle because he is the only one in the story who acknowledges it. It is the riddle of man's existence in his yearning for freedom and self-fulfillment and in the knowledge of his enslavement to the established order.

Let us assume, then, the hypothesis that Gregor's transformation represents a cluster of feelings at the center of which is Gregor's ambivalence—a yearning for freedom from the established order which he does not understand and which he cannot trace back to its original causes, and the feeling that he is as vile as an insect because he does not want to belong to the established order, even though he desires I-thou relationships with individuals in that established order and feels that it is his duty to his family to work within that order. The beetle also represents Gregor's revolt and the established order's revulsion at such a revolt.

So we note that after Gregor's transformation he is "unusually hungry." This hunger theme is developed in much the same way as it is in "The Hunger Artist"—neither Gregor nor the hunger artist knows what food will satisfy his hunger, although Gregor gets a glimpse.

Gregor is repulsed by fresh food and eats the decayed foods which are natural to some insects. However, after Gregor defied his mother and sister and was bombarded with apples by his father, his feelings of hunger for love come to his mind and he thinks how they are neglecting him. . . .

After a description of the sister's increasing neglect of Gregor's room, her quarrel with her mother, and the antics of the charwoman, we learn that "Gregor was hardly eating anything. . . . At first he thought it was chagrin over the state of his room that prevented him from eating, yet he soon got used to the various changes in his room."

The next reference to hunger occurs when Gregor watches the lodgers eating.

> When they were alone again, they ate their food in almost complete silence. It seemed remarkable to Gregor that among the various noises coming from the table he could always distinguish the sound of their masticating teeth, as if this were a sign to Gregor that one needed teeth in order to eat, and that with toothless jaws even of the finest make one could do nothing. "I'm hungry enough," said Gregor sadly to himself, "but not for that kind of food. How these lodgers are stuffing themselves, and here I am dying of starvation."

So it was naturally not food at all that Gregor needed, but an unknown nourishment that he perceives but faintly when he hears his sister play the violin.

> Gregor's sister was playing so beautifully. Her face leaned sideways, intently and sadly her eyes followed the notes of music. Gregor crawled a little farther forward and lowered his head to the ground so that it might be possible for his eyes to meet hers. Was he an animal, that music had such an effect upon him? He felt as if the way were opening before him to the unknown nourishment he craved.

How are we to intellectualize the music as a symbol? Or should we? We remember that Gregor before his transformation did not care for music himself, but was determined to send his sister to the conservatory, even against his parents' wishes. Now he seems to be the only one who truly appreciates Grete's playing, and he is annoyed at the indifference of the lodgers.

A RETURN TO ORDER

His long day-dream that immediately follows deals with an I-thou relationship with his sister. Gregor thinks that for the first time his frightful appearance will become useful to him "for he would protect his sister and appreciate her music as it should be appreciated."

It is important here to note that when Gregor saw and heard his sister play, he *followed his impulse* to enter the living room. "He felt hardly any surprise at his growing lack of consideration for the others; there had been a time when he prided himself on being considerate." Thus, Gregor begins to follow his true impulse toward self-fulfillment in an existential reality which denies the world of mechanized and empty, but functional public order.

However, the world of order cannot tolerate this monstrosity, and Gregor cannot live in an atmosphere of complete rejection. His sister pronounces sentence. "He must go. . . . If this were Gregor, he would have realized long ago that human beings can't live with such a creature and he'd have gone away of his own accord."

It is interesting that Gregor on then returning to his room is astonished at the distance and wonders how he could have crawled so far into the living room without noticing it. The reader knows the reason—he had been receiving the unknown nourishment that he craved.

Just as "The Hunger Artist" ends with the image of the panther with its strong physical existence, unaware of the cage, so *Metamorphosis* concludes with the death of the spiritual and the triumph of the unquestioning physical existence in the established order. At the end of the family's journey into the country, Grete "sprang to her feet first and stretched her young body."

The Metamorphosis Is an Allegorical Beast Fable

Nalini Natarajan

Author and Kafka scholar Nalini Natarajan of the University of Puerto Rico, Rio Piedras discusses *The Metamorphosis* in light of traditional beast fables. In beast fables, metamorphosis is a common technique for depicting a character's altered mental state in metaphorical form. Despite the fact that it allows individuals an opportunity to observe the secrets of everyday life, metamorphosis is feared, reflecting human anxieties about the body, such as uneasiness about sexuality, ugliness, or weakness. Sometimes what one learns through metamorphosis, however, is no more revealing than everyday life; what Gregor discovers through his transformation, for example, is that his life as a salesman parallels the discomfort, isolation, and powerlessness he feels as a bug.

The meanings of metamorphosis and the ways animals are used to examine human anxieties regarding identity, worth, and isolation problematize the very notion of the human, exposing humanity as an uncertain rather than transcendent category.

Metamorphosis can illuminate the limits of the beast fable as a genre. In traditional beast fables all over the world, the boundary maintained between narrative and 'moralitas' corresponds to a separation between animal and human. While animals populate the narrative, the moral clearly refers to the human world. Animals can represent human interactions and wisdom only because the allegorical component of the tale insures an ontological, essential separation between human and beast. . . .

THE BODY

Metamorphosis raises crucial questions about the body and language. The idea of metamorphosis is an ancient one, occurring in myths and fables all over the world. In the broadest sense, any metamorphosis becomes a useful method to depict change of state. . . . It appears that the beast's body gives the individual who has been metamorphosed a chance to "suffer the turns of fate under an animal's skin." Also, the animal can observe the secrets of everyday life because humans are unaware of their presence.

At the same time, the fear of metamorphosis reflects human anxieties about the body: fears of sexuality, ugliness, weakness. Metamorphosis in fairy tales is linked to human powerlessness: witches' curses result in metamorphoses. While voluntary metamorphosis (as in Greek myths) is a measure of the divine, lack of power over the process is a measure of the human. Sometimes, metamorphoses accompany battles between parties. Thus, in a folktale from *The Arabian Nights*, two of the adversaries become, in succession, lions, scorpions, snakes, eagles; each metamorphosis is aimed at gaining greater power. In the Hindu epic, the Ramayana, the hero Rama is tricked by a demon turned deer, Maricha. The subtext of metamorphosis, thus, can be seen as the anxiety accompanying human vulnerability.

METAMORPHOSIS AND LANGUAGE

The power of language to construct, even transform, reality is very relevant here. The point has been made that fables have affinities with proverbs, many of which are often condensed fables. One way of looking at literary metamorphosis is as a fictional representation of metaphor. . . . That is, when we say that someone "monkeys around," we are speaking metaphorically, but when we inscribe this transformation in literal terms, we have a tale of metamorphosis. . . .

This concern with language and the body informs the following reading of Kafka's *Metamorphosis* (1948) . . . Kafka's well known story describes the slow decline and death of a harassed salesman who turns into a giant insect. . . .

Many of the descriptions in Kafka's tale relate the ugliness of the insect body and the pain and discomfort it produces. Gregor's insecthood is graphically described: his hard, armour plated back and the stiff, arched segments of his "dome-like brown belly" cause him discomfort:

However violently he forced himself toward his right side he always toiled on to his back again. He tried it at least a hundred
times shutting his eyes to keep from seeing his struggling legs.

Yet nothing could be more descriptive of the pain of animality
than the passage describing Gregor's death "with the rotting
apple in his back and the inflamed area around it, all covered
with dust."...

HUMAN AND INSECT ARE ONE

The point of contact between human and beast is vulnerability; discomfort of the body is crucial to the metamorphoses. In
Kafka's tale, Gregor's account of his life as a salesman parallels
the discomfort, the irregularity, the isolation and the powerlessness that drain his body as an insect....

The underlying implication of Kafka's narrative is that after
all, there is not that much difference between human and insect; the text negotiates the relationship between a real insect
and a metaphoric one when similar states of mind connect

DOUBLE POSSIBILITY OF INTERPRETATION IN KAFKA

*It is a mistake to try to interpret everything in Kafka in
detail, for in his work, symbols are always in general and
resist a word-for-word rendering.*

The whole art of Kafka consists in forcing the reader to reread.
His endings, or his absence of endings, suggest explanations
which, however, are not revealed in clear language but, before
they seem justified, require that the story be reread from another point of view. Sometimes there is a double possibility of
interpretation, whence appears the necessity for two readings.
This is what the author wanted. But it would be wrong to try to
interpret everything in Kafka in detail. A symbol is always in
general and, however precise its translation, an artist can re-
store to it only its movement: there is no word-for-word rendering. Moreover, nothing is harder to understand than a symbolic
work. A symbol always transcends the one who makes use of it
and makes him say in reality more than he is aware of expressing. In this regard, the surest means of getting hold of it is not
to provoke it, to begin the work without a preconceived attitude
and not to look for its hidden currents. For Kafka in particular it
is fair to agree to his rules, to approach the drama through its
externals and the novel through its form.

Excerpted from "Hope and the Absurd in the Work of Franz Kafka," by Albert
Camus, in *Kafka: A Collection of Critical Essays,* by Ronald Gray. Englewood
Cliffs, NJ: Prentice-Hall, 1965.

human and animal: thus, the exhaustion, futility, loneliness that characterize Gregor's life before he becomes an insect are strangely familiar. The conversation among Gregor (attempting to disguise his metamorphosis), his parents, and the salesman proves as strenuous and frustrating as Gregor's strenuous efforts to adapt to his insecthood. Similarly, Gregor's attempt to support his family, to provide opportunities for his sister, seem futilely counter-productive, since they only engendered laziness in the family. So, too, do his pathetic attempts to move as an insect.

The text's suggestion of the identity of experience between human and insect is partly responsible for the fact that there is no surprise at the thing that has befallen Samsa. Thus, Gregor is angry with the chief clerk for not understanding his predicament: "what had happened to him today might someday happen to the chief clerk; one really could not deny that it was possible."

The *Metamorphosis* Emphasizes a Feminine Mode of Existence

Gerhard Schepers

Writing for *Humanities: Christianity and Culture*, author and Kafka scholar Gerhard Schepers claims that many critics have misinterpreted *The Metamorphosis* because they have based their readings on the cultural tradition of a masculine mode of existence, when much of Kafka's work, and *The Metamorphosis* in particular, instead emphasizes a feminine mode of existence—what psychologist Carl Jung termed *anima*. Illustrated through numerous images in *The Metamorphosis*, *anima* appears as receptivity, flexibility, mutual giving and receiving, and a need to be with others. Living in this feminine mode of existence, Gregor is ultimately forced to give up any sense of individuality in favor of sacrificing his life for the greater good of his family. He retreats to the world of *amae*, accepting his own death and thinking of his family with tenderness and love.

One of the reasons why Kafka is so often misinterpreted is, in my view, similar to the reason why the Japanese, too, are often misunderstood, namely the fact that Western critics in both cases usually base their interpretations on a cultural tradition in which what could be called the 'masculine mode of existence' is strongly emphasized whereas the 'feminine mode of existence' is, to a high degree though not completely, suppressed. The distinction made here between the masculine and the feminine modes of existence is related to C.G. Jung's distinction between *animus* and *anima*, the 'male' and the 'female' soul. The masculine mode of existence can be characterized as detachment, tension, action, achievement, striving,

From "Images of *Amae* in Kafka," by Gerhard Schepers, *Humanities: Christianity and Culture*, July 1980. Reprinted with permission from the author.

creativity, responsibility, determination, will, duty; the feminine mode of existence as receptivity, flexibility, conservation, mutual giving and receiving, embracing, oneness, being-with-others. Both are not confined to men or women respectively, but they are possible modes of existence for both sexes, though men may have a predisposition to the masculine and women to the feminine mode, a difficult question which cannot be discussed here. What is important is the fact that for the development of man's personality both modes of existence are necessary, that they have to be integrated. Where this is not achieved the masculine mode is in danger of becoming one-sided rationalism, legalism, and so on, and the feminine mode would then become or remain blind nature. Whereas the masculine mode of existence predominates in the West, in Japan and, interestingly, to some extent also in Kafka, the feminine mode of existence is emphasized. . . . This will be demonstrated in the following by what is an essential element in the feminine mode of existence, namely the psychology of *amae*, which has been described by Takeo Doi in his book *The Anatomy of Dependence* and in other publications.

The word *amae* is the noun form of the verb *amaeru*, which, according to Doi, means: "to depend and presume upon another's benevolence". It has the same root as the adjective *amai*, which means "sweet". Thus *amaeru* has a distinct feeling of sweetness and is generally used to describe a child's attitude or behavior toward his parents, particularly his mother. But it can also be used to describe the relationship between two adults, such as the relationship between a husband and a wife or a master and a subordinate. I believe that there is no single word in English equivalent to *amaeru*, though this does not mean that the psychology of *amae* is totally alien to the people of English speaking countries.

Amae, in children, refers to their feeling of dependence, the desire to be passively loved, the unwillingness to be separated from the warm mother-child circle and confronted with objective reality. But in Japan, to a far greater extent than in the West, *amae* also shapes the relationship between adults. As John Bester says in the foreword to *The Anatomy of Dependence:* "On the personal level, this means that within his own most intimate circle, and to diminishing degrees outside that circle, he (i.e. the adult Japanese) seeks relationships that, however binding they may be in their outward aspects, allow him to presume, as it were, on familiarity. For him, the assurance of another person's good will permits a certain degree of self-indulgence, and a corresponding degree of indifference to the claims of the other person as a separate individual. Such a relationship implies a considerable blurring of the distinction between subject and object; as such, it is not necessarily governed by what might be considered strict rational or moral standards, and may often seem selfish to the outsider. Sometimes even, the individual may deliberately act in a way that is childish as a sign to the other that he . . . wishes to be dependent and seeks the other's 'indulgence'."

Whereas such an attitude is socially sanctioned in Japan, in adults in the West it is usually regarded as 'childish' and therefore suppressed. It seems to be incompatible with the idea of the self-reliant, free, and responsible personality.

This basic psychological difference between Japan and the West explains why the Japanese language could develop a large vocabulary relating to *amaeru* by which even subtle differences of the various forms of *amaeru* or of disappointed *amae* can be described, whereas modern Western languages have only a few terms to express some, usually negative, aspects of this psychology, and no word for *amaeru*, the central element in all these emotions. . . .

. . . The images of *amae* in *Metamorphosis*, which, although they are only one aspect of this highly complex story, nevertheless play a crucial role in it, for it deals mainly with human relations and these are almost all, to a varying degree, determined by the psychology of *amae*.

GREGOR'S WISH TO BE CARED FOR

The central image in *Metamorphosis* is that of the insect or beetle, into which Gregor Samsa is transformed. The narrative begins with the words:

> As Gregor Samsa awoke one morning from uneasy dreams he found himself transformed in his bed into a gigantic insect. He was lying on his hard, as it were armor-plated, back and when he lifted his head a little he could see his domelike brown belly divided into stiff arched segments on top of which the bed quilt could hardly keep in position and was about to slide off completely. His numerous legs, which were pitifully thin compared to the rest of his bulk, waved helplessly before his eyes.
>
> What has happened to me? he thought. It was no dream.

The transformation is introduced without any further explanations just as a fact which we have to accept. And so does

Gregor with the words: "It was no dream". Though later he will again and again try to deny this fact or at least to avoid facing its obvious consequences.

It should be pointed out here that in *Metamorphosis* we are never given an objective description of reality, but throughout the story we see almost everything only through the eyes of the protagonist, even to some extent at the end of the story when Gregor has already died. Accordingly Kafka no longer uses quotation marks, as he did in his earlier stories, to distinguish what Gregor says to himself from the rest of the narrative. Everything is an expression of the subjective consciousness of the protagonist, though this may also include the viewpoints of others which he takes over because he is dependent on them. It would be interesting to compare this feature of Kafka's narratives with similar phenomena in Japanese language and culture, but this would lead too far away from the topic of this paper which concentrates on what is an essential element in both, namely the psychology and vocabulary of *amae*.

Returning now to the first sentences of the story we can find there already an indication of the double-meaning of Gregor's transformation: the hard, armor-plated back and the stiff, arched segments of his domelike belly contrast with his pitifully thin, helplessly waving legs. The weakness and helplessness of the protagonist indicated by the latter is emphasized throughout the story. As an insect he can now, like a baby, no longer be responsible for his own life, the family has to take care of him and must feed him. That this corresponds to his inner wish to *amaeru*, to presume on others, to be cared for, is illustrated by many instances in the story. When, for instance, he tries hard to get out of bed and has finally rocked himself into a position where it is very easy to get out just by letting himself fall he is suddenly struck by the idea of how nice it would be if his family came and would lift him out of bed like a baby.

In the *Letter to his Father* Kafka has his father argue against him by saying: "Why should it bother you that you are unfit for life, since I have the responsibility for it, while you calmly stretch out and let yourself be hauled through life, physically and mentally by me."

Whenever Gregor's family fails to care for him sufficiently, as he sees it, he complains about it in a form which is typical of disappointed *amae*. Once when his sister has brought him food which he does not like he thinks: ". . . would she bring in some other kind of food more to his taste? If she did not do it of her own accord, he would rather starve than draw her attention to the fact, although he felt a wild impulse to dart out from under the sofa, throw himself at her feet and beg her for something to eat." This attitude of, on the one side, being willing to starve and, on the other, feeling a wild impulse to implore his sister for something to eat would be paradoxical or absurd if he were only interested in the food, but what he obviously really longs for is his sister's care, and this he expresses in two different forms of *amae*. In Japanese the former could be called *hinekureru* (to behave in a distorted way), which according to Doi means "feigning indifference to the other instead of showing *amae*. Under the surface one is, in fact, concerned with the other's reaction." The latter, in Japanese, can be called *tanomu* (to ask, to beg, to implore, to rely on), which according to Doi is also a form of *amae*. The reference to the vocabulary of *amae* thus makes it clear that both seemingly inconsistent attitudes are actually only two different forms of one basic attitude, namely *amae*. The phrase "throw himself at her feet" ironically corresponds to what Gregor already expresses by his low body, which is always 'at the feet' of others; it expresses submissiveness, another feature of *amae*. In this way Gregor looks up to his mother calling her name in a low voice and similarly even before his transformation he had looked up to his chief.

The German word to describe Gregor's movements as an insect is *kriechen* which means "to creep, to crawl", but also "to cringe, to crawl on all fours before a person". Again Gregor's physical appearance and actions express his mental attitude which we notice especially when he speaks to the chief clerk.

In this way his insect-body and its 'gestures' are an expression of *amae*, but at the same time the very fact that he has been transformed into an insect means that he is excluded from human community and therefore also from the world of *amae*. The image of the insect thus, on the one side, expresses Gregor's strong wish to be allowed to *amaeru*, and, on the other side, it shows the impossibility of *amae*. Furthermore it also demonstrates different forms of disappointed *amae*.

As a beetle Gregor turns his back—which moreover is armor-plated—on other people, thus indicating that he would like to keep them away from him; he has hardened in his relation to other people. This also corresponds to the fact that he has the habit of locking the three doors to the rooms of his parents and his sister during the night. In the vocabulary of *amae* this attitude is described as *kodawaru* (to obstruct, to oppose, to stick to), *futekusareru* (to become sulky) or *suneru* (to be sulky). The latter attitude Gregor expresses also when, after his room has once been cleaned against his will, he demonstrates his anger through what one might call a 'gesture' of his body lying "widespread, sulky and motionless on the sofa". Several times in the text Gregor is called "obstinate", which corresponds to the Japanese *kodawaru*. The German word is *hartnäckig* which literally means "hard-necked" and thus again corresponds to his physical appearance.

A typical expression of disappointed *amae* in Japan is the so-called *higaisha ishiki* (sense of being victimized). Gregor demonstrates by his flat body how much he is weighed down by the heavy burden he has to carry for his family, and even after his death his "completely flat and dry" body expresses this *higaisha ishiki*.

Closely related to the psychology of *amae* is the feeling of shame, which, similarly to what Ruth Benedict has pointed out with regard to Japanese culture, plays a very important role in Kafka. This corresponds to Gregor's instincts as an insect which make him hide under the sofa whenever someone enters the room.

OTHER INSTANCES OF *AMAE* IN *METAMORPHOSIS*

In the following I shall try to illustrate what has been discussed above by further examples of *amae* in *Metamorphosis*.

At the beginning of the story there is a situation where Gregor, in a desperate attempt to retain his job, is trying to open the door of his room in order to attend to business, and while doing so he thinks:

> . . . he was eager to find out what the others, after all their insistence, would say at the sight of him.

This sentence shows that he still refuses to analyze his own situation objectively, for in that case he should know, of course, what the others would say at the sight of him. Instead, he makes his own evaluation of the situation completely dependent on their reaction. The word "insistence" does not well render the meaning of the German *"nach ihm verlangen"*, which can either mean "to long for him" or "to ask for him, to demand that he should appear". The latter obviously expresses their real attitude (and in this sense the translation is correct), but Gregor, as for instance the following passage in the text shows, is apparently inclined to believe that the others long for him and so respond to his *amaeru.*

> If they were horrified then the responsibility was no longer his and he could stay quiet. But if they took it calmly, then he had no reason either to be upset, and could really get to the station for the eight o'clock train if he hurried.

This seemingly rational reflection is, of course, absurd if taken as such. It only demonstrates the uselessness of this kind of thought. From the point of view of *amae,* however, it is quite consistent. If the others are horrified, that means if they consider him an insect, then he has no more responsibility, like a baby, and they have to care for him. But if they take it calmly then—so much is he dependent on their opinion—he thinks he can continue to live as before.

The reaction of his family is, of course, that they are horrified; they seem to realize that "some great misfortune" must have happened. His mother calls for the doctor, his father for the locksmith to open the door to Gregor's room. Gregor's reaction corresponds to what he has said before: they have taken over the responsibility, and to he is calm, inspite of his desperate situation:

> Yet at any rate people now believed that something was wrong with him, and were ready to help him. The positive certainty with which these first measures had been taken comforted him. He felt himself drawn once more into the human circle and hoped for great and remarkable results from both the doctor and the locksmith, without really distinguishing precisely between them.

The last sentence ironically shows what kind of irrational hopes Gregor has once he feels himself drawn into the warm world of *amae.*

Throughout the story we find many examples of two typical ways of expressing disappointed *amae,* namely *higaisha ishiki* (sense of being a victim, consciousness of having been wronged) and *higaiteki ni uketoru* (to take something—often mistakenly—as an attack on or criticism of oneself). Related to these there is an abundance of expressions in Japanese to indicate the concrete fact of *higai,* of receiving harm. The Japanese language even possesses its specific grammatical mode, the so-called passive, to express the *higaisha ishiki,* for instance if one says *asobiba ni ie o taterarete shimatta* (someone—to our dismay—went and built a house on our playground).

Examples of this mentality are particularly abundant in a passage where Gregor's reaction is described when his mother and sister begin to remove the furniture from his room. At first, it seems that he has no objections to it, but then he becomes more and more irritated and obviously can no longer control his feelings.

> ... he soon had to admit that all this trotting to and fro of the two women, their little ejaculations, and the scraping of furniture along the floor affected him like a vast disturbance coming from all sides at once, and however much he tucked in his head and legs and cowered to the very floor he was bound to confess that he would not be able to stand it for long.

Almost physically he feels what they are doing to him by "clearing his room out; taking away everything he loved". They even try to remove his writing desk "which had almost sunk into the floor", literally: "which was already firmly buried / dug into the ground / floor" (German: *schon im Boden fest eingegraben*"). This expression is typical of Kafka's style. It is, of course, not an objective description, but an expression of Gregor's feelings. It shows how much he clings to the desk and how much it hurts him when they violently, as he sees it, try to remove it.

So he rushes out and, not knowing what to rescue first, finally clings to a picture of a lady in fur. "This picture at least, which entirely hidden beneath him, was going to be removed by nobody". This attitude can be characterized in the Japanese vocabulary of *amae* by the verb *kodawaru* (to obstruct, to oppose, to stick to).

When his mother and sister come back "Grete had twined her arm around her mother and was almost supporting her". What Gregor expects from his sister she is instead showing to his mother, namely tender care and affection. She is almost "carrying" (German: "*tragen*") her as Gregor had wished his family to do with him. How much he is frustrated by the fact that he is excluded from this warm human relationship, is expressed in the next sentences:

> Her intentions were clear enough to Gregor, she wanted to bestow her mother in safety and then chase him down from the wall. Well, just let her try it! He clung to his picture and would not give it up. He would rather fly in Grete's face.

His *kodawaru*, his clinging to the picture, and his determination to oppose any attempt to take it away from him, combines with *shunen* (evil attachment, spite, vindictive feelings). The latter is, according to Doi, often accompanied by delusions of persecution as well as grandeur, demonstrated here by Gregor's belief that his sister will "chase him down from the wall" and, on the other hand, by his threat to rather fly in her face than to let the picture go.

RETURNING TO THE WORLD OF *AMAE*

Similar instances of disappointed *amae* we find in a passage near the end of the story where Gregor observes how the three lodgers who are now living with them are treated by the family in a way he had always wished to be treated. Whereas he is excluded now from family life, they have taken his place. Everything his parents and sister do to them seems to him a rejection of his own wish to *amaeru*. The detailed description of their (in Gregor's view) exaggerated obligingness and submissiveness shows his growing irritation. Thus what is described here is again not an objective account but an expression of Gregor's feelings, his *higamu* (to become jaundiced, prejudiced, feel oneself unfairly treated) and even *uramu* (to show resentment or hatred as a result of disappointed *amae*). This is mixed with a feeling of shame at the fact that his family has to behave in this submissive way because he no longer supports them.

> It seemed remarkable to Gregor that among the various noises coming from the table he could always distinguish the sound of their masticating teeth, as if this were a sign to Gregor that one needed teeth in order to eat, and that with toothless jaws even of the finest make one could do nothing.

This is a good example of *higaiteki ni uketoru* (to take something—often mistakenly—as an attack on or criticism of oneself) mentioned already above as an expression of disappointed *amae*. The lodgers do not know of his existence, so it is clearly only in his own imagination, as an expression of his feeling of disappointed *amae*, that they seem to demonstrate the efficiency of their masticating teeth to him.

The climax of Gregor's frustration is reached when the lodgers invite his sister, who had remained closest to him in the family, to their room to play the violin there, whereas Gregor is left alone in his room full of junk. At this point he flees into wishful, sentimental and fairy-tale like dreams, hoping that his sister will agree to live with him in his room. He imagines that music could be the common bond between them, though it had been clearly stated before that, unlike his sister, he did not love music. Turning away from reality where he can no longer find the fulfilment out of his wish to *amaeru* he clings to irrational hopes of a kind of redemption through music: "He felt as if the way were opening before him to the unknown nourishment he craved." His delusions of persecution as well as grandeur are demonstrated by his intention "to watch all the doors of his room at once and spit at intruders", like a dragon using his "frightful appearance" to deter them. Finally, completely neglecting the fact that he is an insect now he imagines a sentimental and romantic scene where his sister, sitting beside him on the sofa, "would be so touched that she would burst into tears, and Gregor would then raise himself to her shoulder and kiss her on the neck."

These illusions are abruptly destroyed when he is discovered by the lodgers. He is now finally excluded from the world of human beings and has to realize that there is only one possibility left to return to the world of *amae*, the same possibility that is also offered in Japan in a similar desperate situation, namely to die for the sake of the family or group and in this way to be re-united with them, though it means to give up any claim to an individual existence. Thus Gregor, the night before his death, resigning himself to his fate, feels "relatively comfortable", though his whole body is aching. He thinks of his family with "tenderness and love", although they have excluded him from their circle and caused his death. He completely agrees with them and, in this sense, is now re-united with them, though this means that he has to accept his own death. "The decision that he must disappear was one that he held to even more strongly than his sister, if that were possible."

CHRONOLOGY

1883

Franz Kafka is born in Prague, Czechoslovakia, on July 3.

1889–1893

Kafka attends German elementary school.

1893–1901

Kafka attends German preparatory school at the German State Gymnasium. During this time he begins writing his own prose sketches.

1896

Kafka celebrates his bar mitzvah.

1901–1906

Kafka begins formal studies of German literature and law at the German Karl-Ferdinand University in Prague. He also spends some time in Munich.

1902

Kafka meets Max Brod, who would later become his biographer.

1904–1905

Kafka writes "Description of a Struggle."

1905–1906

Kafka works as an unpaid probationer in the law office of Richard Löwy in Prague. After receiving his doctorate at law, he begins practical training in the Prague criminal and civil courts.

1907–1908

Kafka writes "Wedding Preparations in the Country."

1908

Kafka takes a position at the semigovernmental Workers' Accident Insurance Institute.

1909

Two sections of "Description of a Struggle" are published in *Hyperion*.

1910

Kafka develops an interest in Yiddish theater. He begins writing his diaries and writes the first draft of *Amerika*. Kafka travels to Paris and Berlin.

1911

Kafka has contact with a Yiddish theater company and forms a friendship with actor Isaac Löwy; he begins a study of Jewish folklore. His travels include trips with Max Brod to Switzerland, Italy, and France. Kafka writes travel diaries during this time.

1912

Kafka meets and begins a correspondence with Felice Bauer from Berlin. He writes *The Judgement, The Metamorphosis,* and completes the first seven chapters of *Amerika*.

1913

The first of Kafka's book publications, *Meditation*, appears in January as a collection of small vignettes, meditations, and impressions. "The Stoker" and *The Judgement* are also published. He visits Felice Bauer in Berlin and also travels to Vienna and Italy.

1914

Kafka writes "Memoirs of the Kalda Railroad" and "In the Penal Colony," and begins writing *The Trial*. He becomes engaged to Felice Bauer, but the engagement is broken off during the year. After moving from his parents' home, Kafka meets Grete Bloch. He also travels to Germany.

1915

Kafka reconnects with Felice Bauer, continues working on *The Trial,* and receives the Fontane Prize for "The Stoker." *The Metamorphosis* is published and he writes "The Village Schoolmaster." Grete Bloch allegedly gives birth to Kafka's son, unbeknownst to him.

1917

Kafka and Felice Bauer become engaged for the second time, but the wedding plans are dissolved after five months. After being diagnosed with tuberculosis, Kafka takes a leave of absence from work and moves to the country with his sister Ottla, where he writes numerous stories and parables, including "The Great Wall of China," "A Country Doctor," "The New Attorney," and others.

1918

Kafka writes "The Bucket-Rider," continues to work on his parables, and returns to Prague to work half-time at the insurance institute. He meets Julie Wohryzek. His health continues to decline and he requires intermittent stays at various sanatoria.

1919

Kafka resumes work on his diary entries, and writes "Letter to His Father." "In the Penal Colony," and "A Country Doctor" are published, and he writes a collection of aphorisms. He and Julie Wohryzek get engaged, but the engagement is broken in November.

1920

Kafka takes a sick leave from the Workers' Accident Insurance Institute; he meets and falls in love with Czech writer Milena Jesenská-Pollak, and writes the first draft of *The Castle*.

1921

Kafka returns to work at the Workers' Accident Insurance Institute. "The Bucket Rider" is published.

1922

Kafka's medical condition worsens, and he asks Max Brod to destroy his work after his death. He retires from the insurance institute, completes *The Castle* and writes *A Hunger Artist*, "Investigations of a Dog," and "On Parables." Kafka has a final meeting with Milena Jesenská-Pollak in which he breaks off his relations with her.

1923

Kafka lives in Berlin with new girlfriend Dora Dymant; he writes "The Burrow," and "Josephine the Singer."

1924

Kafka moves back to Prague. He dies on June 3 at Kierling Sanatorium near Vienna and is buried on June 11 in the Jewish cemetery in Prague. His short-story collection, *A Hunger Artist* is published soon after his death.

FOR FURTHER RESEARCH

BIOGRAPHY

Max Brod, *Franz Kafka: A Biography*. New York: Da Capo Press, 1995.

Michael Carrouges, *Kafka Versus Kafka*. Tuscaloosa: University of Alabama Press, 1968.

Sander L. Gilman, *Franz Kafka, the Jewish Patient*. New York: Routledge, 1995.

Ronald Gray, *Franz Kafka*. London: Cambridge University Press, 1973.

Frederick R. Karl, *Franz Kafka, Representative Man*. New York: Ticknor & Fields, 1991.

Anthony Northey, *Kafka's Relatives: Their Lives and His Writing*. New Haven: Yale University Press, 1991.

Ernst Pawel, *The Nightmare of Reason: A Life of Franz Kafka*. New York: Farrar, Straus, and Giroux, 1992.

Walter Sokel, *Franz Kafka*. New York: Columbia University Press, 1966.

CRITICISM

Raymond Armstrong, *Kafka and Pinter: Shadow-Boxing: The Struggle Between Father and Son*. New York: St. Martin's Press, 1999.

Steven Berkoff, *Meditations on Metamorphosis*. Boston: Faber and Faber, 1995.

Harold Bloom, ed., *Modern Critical Interpretations: The Metamorphosis*. New York: Chelsea House, 1988.

——, Harold Bloom, ed., *Modern Critical Views: Franz Kafka*. New York: Chelsea House, 1986.

Elizabeth Boa, *Kafka: Gender, Class and Race in the Letters and Fictions*. New York: Oxford University Press, 1996.

Kurt J. Fickert, *End of a Mission: Kafka's Search for Truth in His Last Stories*. Rochester, NY: Camden House, 1993.

Angel Flores and Homer Swander, *Franz Kafka Today*. Madison: University of Wisconsin Press, 1964.

Richard T. Gray, ed., *Approaches to Teaching Kafka's Short Fiction.* New York: Modern Language Association of America, 1995.

Calvin S. Hall and Richard E. Lind, eds., *Dreams, Life, and Literature: A Study of Franz Kafka.* Chapel Hill: University of North Carolina Press, 1970.

Arnold Heidsieck, *The Intellectual Contexts of Kafka's Fiction: Philosophy, Law, Religion.* Columbia, SC: Camden House, 1994.

Kenneth Hughes, ed., *Franz Kafka: An Anthology of Marxist Criticism.* Hanover, NH: University Press of New England, 1981.

Franz R. Kempf, *Everyone's Darling: Kafka and the Critics of His Short Fiction.* Columbia, SC: Camden House, 1994.

William Kluback, *Franz Kafka: Challenges and Confrontations.* New York: P. Lang, 1993.

Richard H. Lawson, *Franz Kafka.* New York: Ungar, 1987.

Jack Murray, *The Landscapes of Alienation: Ideological Subversion in Kafka, Céline, and Onetti.* Stanford, CA: Stanford University Press, 1991.

Roy Pascal, *Kafka's Narrators: A Study of His Stories and Sketches.* London: Cambridge University Press, 1982.

Roman Struc and J.C. Yardley, *Franz Kafka (1883–1983): His Craft and Thought.* Calgary: Wilfrid Laurier University Press, 1986.

Allen Thiher, *Franz Kafka: A Study of the Short Fiction.* Boston: Twayne, 1990.

Ruth Tiefenbrun, *Moment of Torture: An Interpretation of Franz Kafka's Short Stories.* Carbondale: Southern Illinois University Press, 1973.

TWENTIETH-CENTURY GERMAN LITERATURE AND CULTURE

Elizabeth Boa, *A German Dream: Regional Loyalties and National Identity in German Culture, 1890–1990.* New York: Oxford University Press, 2000.

Deborah Vietor Engländer, ed., *The Legacy of Exile: Lives, Letters, Literature.* Malden, MA: Blackwell, 1998.

Linda E. Feldman and Diana Orendi, eds., *Evolving Jewish Identities in German Culture: Borders and Crossings.* Westport, CT: Praeger, 2000.

Elke P. Frederiksen and Martha Kaarsberg Wallach, eds., *Facing Fascism and Confronting the Past: German Women Writers from Weimar to the Present.* Albany: State University of New York Press, 2000.

Mary Fulbrook and Martin Swales, *Representing the German Nation: History and Identity in Twentieth-Century Germany.* New York: Manchester University Press, 2000.

Raymond Furness, *Zarathustra's Children: A Study of a Lost Generation of German Writers.* Rochester, NY: Camden House, 2000.

Noah William Isenberg, *Between Redemption and Doom: The Strains of German-Jewish Modernism.* Lincoln: University of Nebraska Press, 1999.

Carol Poore, *The Bonds of Labor: German Journeys to the Working World, 1890–1990.* Detroit: Wayne State University Press, 2000.

TWENTIETH-CENTURY JEWISH LITERATURE

Randolph L. Braham, *Reflections of the Holocaust in Art and Literature.* New York: Columbia University Press, 1990.

Ezra Mendelsohn, *Literary Strategies: Jewish Texts and Contexts.* New York: Oxford University Press, 1996.

Gershon Shaked, *The Shadows Within: Essays on Modern Jewish Writers.* Philadelphia: Jewish Publication Society, 1987.

Maurice Wohlgelernter, ed., *Jewish Writers/Irish Writers: Selected Essays on the Love of Words.* New Brunswick, NJ: Transaction Publishers, 2000.

Leon I. Yudkin, *Jewish Writing and Identity in the Twentieth Century.* New York: St. Martin's Press, 1982.

INDEX